'Jacqui Pretty has produced a superb, step-b~
for any entrepreneur who want~
down to share with the world, ᴇ
through the "author-ity" that ha

This is an easy-to-read, well-　　　　　　　structured book that takes you by the han　　 ＿ɴu guides you step by step, exercise by exercise, to develop a detailed, "better than average" plan for your book. Once you have developed this to completion it will be – as Jacqui promises – just about as if the book will write itself.

I highly recommend this tome to anyone who wants to take their business to the next level and become recognised as an authority in their field.'

Geoff Hetherington, JG Hetherington – The Clarity CEO

Book Blueprint is a guide that every entrepreneur needs. It is your friend when the decisions are too hard (like 'should my book be a how-to book, a thought leadership book, or a book of lists?'). It is a step-by-step pragmatic partner when you're stuck. It is a foil to the crazy trap so many entrepreneurs fall into of too many ideas and too little action. If you want to write a book, and you keep getting waylaid by the next shiny idea, this is your moment of "done". *Book Blueprint* helped me make choices in my writing journey that will support my business and provide the answers my audience wants. The clarity it provided is invaluable.'

Rosemary Shapiro-Liu, Triple Win Enterprises

Book Blueprint provides a framework that reduces the stress new authors feel at tackling such a monumental task. Jacqui chunks it down into little bite-sized bits that readers can work through one at a time.'

Crystal Fieldhouse, Ecology Skincare

'Jacqui Pretty's book was just the helping hand I needed. Applying her action steps allowed me to confidently take a half-finished, stagnant mess of a book and turn it into a beautifully written masterpiece that I can be proud of. Her structured approach showed me how to organise my thoughts and knowledge and has made writing quality content quick and effortless. I'm so grateful!'

Diana Popov, *Skin Deep Australia*

'I love this book! After more than two years spent floundering, I finally feel like I have enough structure in place to actually start writing. Before I was jumping from idea to idea and didn't have any kind of plan or flow. But after reading *Book Blueprint* and undertaking the exercises, I think I may just be able to crack this thing!'

Alanna Quigley, *Baby Babble*

'This book is brilliant. Although I had all my chapters pretty clear I kept feeling there was something missing. I knew I could write the book from here, but what *Book Blueprint* has shown me is so much easier. I'm so grateful.'

Sarah McCrum, *Sarah McCrum*

'I found this book at an opportune time. My book *Apps for Patients: A 6-step guide for health professionals* was written and had been to an editor, but I felt something was not gelling and that it did not hold together as well as it could. *Book Blueprint* gave me guidance to structure the content in a way that was logical, made sense and, most of all, was readable for my audience. By implementing even some of the ideas in *Book Blueprint*, I was able to write a better book that would be read, understood and enable health care professionals to create apps that can save lives.'

Julie Mission, *Make it APPen*

'As an editor who works with entrepreneurs to get their books out into the world, I'm thrilled to see Jacqui Pretty's *Book Blueprint* released. Full of comprehensive, easy-to-follow guidance, I recommend it to anyone who wants to discover the secret to producing a book that will raise their profile and set them apart from their peers.'

Sara Litchfield, *Right Ink on the Wall*

'Jacqui Pretty's *Book Blueprint* is filled with great ideas and processes that helped get the stuff swirling around in my head out on paper. I loved getting out the coloured pens to create my initial mind maps and particularly liked the way the book has clearly marked action steps throughout each chapter.

I can easily see that second and subsequent books using this method will be even easier as I'll be able to jump back to the action steps and only re-read sections where I need a bit more of a jog.'

Desley Cowley, *Spruiker Hire*

'If you are planning to write your first book (or even your tenth!) do yourself a favour and spend time upfront with Jacqui Pretty's *Book Blueprint*. It is jam-packed with ideas to get you on the right track, especially if you are one of those very right-brained touchy feely entrepreneurs like me! One of the biggest benefits for me was in deciding what style of book I wanted to write. I now go forward with fewer fears and greater confidence.'

Annette Baulch, *Oz Tantra*

Book Blueprint is truly incredible. This book has helped me come out of the fog and confusion in writing my book. The step-by-step action points have allowed me to create a full and complete structure of my book that makes writing so simple and easy.'

Sharanya Naidoo, *Three Cups Full*

'*Book Blueprint* is a must-read book for any entrepreneur looking to write a book, but not sure where or how to start. With clear steps and guidance on how to approach the process of writing, any entrepreneur will find the process easy following Jacqui's approach. This is an easy-to-read book with practical take-aways that can be implemented today.'

Rebecca Coomes, *Coomes Marketing*

'*Book Blueprint* is SERIOUSLY AWESOME. In four days, I went from dithering and procrastinating about a book to understanding my own ideas, organising them into something coherent and feeling absolutely confident that I can write a good, useful book. Get your hands on a copy ASAP.'

Kathryn Logan, *kathlogan.com*

METICULOUS TITLE

BOOK BLUEPRINT

HOW ANY ENTREPRENEUR CAN WRITE AN
AWESOME BOOK

CATCHY SUBTITLE

EXPERIENCED AND KNOWLEDGEABLE AUTHOR

JACQUI PRETTY

NEW YORK

NASHVILLE • MELBOURNE • VANCOUVER

BOOK BLUEPRINT

HOW ANY ENTREPRENEUR CAN WRITE AN AWESOME BOOK

© 2017 Jacqui Pretty

All rights reserved. No portion of this book may be reproduced, stored in a retrieval system, or transmitted in any form or by any means—electronic, mechanical, photocopy, recording, scanning, or other,—except for brief quotations in critical reviews or articles, without the prior written permission of the publisher.

Published in New York, New York, by Morgan James Publishing. Morgan James and The Entrepreneurial Publisher are trademarks of Morgan James, LLC. www.MorganJamesPublishing.com

The Morgan James Speakers Group can bring authors to your live event. For more information or to book an event visit The Morgan James Speakers Group at www.TheMorganJamesSpeakersGroup.com.

Shelfie

A **free** eBook edition is available with the purchase of this print book.

ISBN 978-1-68350-229-6 paperback
ISBN 978-1-68350-230-2 casebound
ISBN 978-1-68350-231-9 eBook
Library of Congress Control Number:
2016915263

CLEARLY PRINT YOUR NAME ABOVE IN UPPER CASE

Instructions to claim your free eBook edition:
1. Download the Shelfie app for Android or iOS
2. Write your name in **UPPER CASE** above
3. Use the Shelfie app to submit a photo
4. Download your eBook to any device

Cover & Interior Design by:
Scarlett Rugers

Cover & Interior Setup by:
Megan Whitney
Creative Ninja Designs
megan@creativeninjadesigns.com

In an effort to support local communities, raise awareness and funds, Morgan James Publishing donates a percentage of all book sales for the life of each book to Habitat for Humanity Peninsula and Greater Williamsburg.

Get involved today! Visit
www.MorganJamesBuilds.com

BOOK BLUEPRINT

*This is dedicated to all of my wonderful clients —
thank you for allowing me to be a part of your
publishing journey.*

Contents

PART 2: THE RIGHT STRUCTURE

PART 3: THE RIGHT CONTENT

PART 4: THE RIGHT LANGUAGE

GRAMMAR GREMLIN

This book has been professionally edited and proofread.
However, sometimes typos can slip through the cracks.
Please note that I take these very seriously, so if you
find any errors, email the Grammar Factory team at
info@grammarfactory.com and we'll send you a free
Grammar Gremlin as a thank you.

Having written a lot of books and helped many entrepreneurs to write their own book, I've either made every mistake imaginable or seen others make them. Writing a book is not that complicated. Writing a great book is. This is where Jacqui Pretty leaps in.

Jacqui and I have worked together on the leading entrepreneurial programme in the world, 'Key Person of Influence', a forty-week incubator for aspiring entrepreneurs to build their profile and stand out from their competitors. One of the best ways to do this is to write and publish an excellent book.

Jacqui has been providing editing services to our aspiring authors. From the start it was pretty darn clear that she had a lot of passion directed at helping these people to not just write a book, but to write the very best book that they could.

In *Book Blueprint* Jacqui starts with this exact premise. After all, what is the point of writing a terrible book? And the harsh reality is that a lot of self-published books are really badly written – well intentioned by all means, but poorly executed.

Jacqui dives deep into the topics that are important, gently coaching the new author through a process that will help them to avoid the most common mistakes, and helping them bit by bit to come to the realisation that they are in fact going to write their book and it is going to be a great one.

I consider Jacqui to be one of those people who is the perfect blend of technical and inspirational. When working through *Book Blueprint* the reader will get all of the technical knowledge that they need, along with practical information and encouragement. One key element that shines through consistently is that this material is delivered at exactly the right time, just as the reader is starting to think about what's next.

Bottom line: If you have always wanted to write your own book, but struggled to find the process, or the detail that you need to get those words out in a way that will reinforce your authority and expertise as an entrepreneur, *Book Blueprint* will go a long way to helping you achieve your dream.

Andrew Griffiths
Australia's #1 Small Business and Entrepreneurial Author –
with 12 books sold in over 60 countries.

How to become the author-ity in your industry

In every industry there are two types of people.

The first are the industry authorities. These people are widely recognised and respected. They are able to pick and choose their work. They get paid more for their services. They book out well in advance. They are the first ones journalists contact for commentary. They are sought-after keynote speakers, and charge premium rates for engagements.

Ultimately, they are the most well-known and well-connected players in their industry. Because of this they are highly valued and they do business on their own terms. While business still has its challenges, it's never a struggle.

The second group are the wannabes. The wannabes *want* to get paid more. They *want* speaking gigs and media appearances. They *want* to turn down undesirable projects so they can focus on doing the work they love for the clients they love.

Unfortunately, the wannabes rarely get what they want. Their days are consumed by client work, enquiries, quotes and prospecting. If they have a team, they also run meetings, coach, answer questions and review their work, hoping that one day – *someday* – their team will grow up and be independent.

They still hold the dream of being an industry authority, so if they get a spare moment they turn to marketing – they update their Facebook status, upload a photo to Instagram, tweak their website or write a blog post... but none of it seems to make a difference. In the end, every attempt they make to establish themselves as an authority just adds to their to-do list, and suddenly it's 2am, and they realise they haven't eaten. And the only thing left in the fridge is a wedge of cheese turning a suspicious shade of green.

So, how do you make the transition from being a wannabe to being an authority?

From wannabe to author-ity

As an editor who has helped over 100 entrepreneurs turn their knowledge and experience into published books, I've seen entrepreneurs become Amazon bestselling authors, land highly paid speaking gigs, get featured on national TV and double their rates, all because they published a book.

Why does this happen?

Because being a published author makes you stand out from the crowd. With the number of small business owners around the globe expected to hit one billion by 2020[1], there are probably thousands, if not millions, of entrepreneurs offering similar services to you and marketing them in similar ways to you. In a world where there are more competitors in the market than ever before, what better way to stand out than becoming a published author?

A published book earns you instant credibility and establishes you as a leader in your industry. While anyone can bluff their way through a blog post, the media, potential clients and potential partners all recognise that you need knowledge and real-world experience to write a book, and will consider you an expert once you're published.

And once you achieve this status, you can expect the opportunities and advantages that come with being an expert...

- 34% of published entrepreneurs double their rates, regardless of whether they have start-ups or mature businesses when they publish.

- 81% of them are featured in the media, including 10% who appear on national TV!

---

1   Anna Vital, 'The Next Billion – Women Entrepreneurs', *Funders and Founders*, January 7, 2013, http://fundersandfounders.com/the-next-billion-women-entrepreneurs.

- 72% of published entrepreneurs get paid speaking engagements, even if they have never been paid to speak before.

- 74% of them find new referral partners.

- 26% of them forge partnerships with the big brands in their industries.

While all of this sounds impressive, did these opportunities make a tangible difference to their businesses? When I reached out to my network of published entrepreneurs, the answer was a resounding 'yes!' Eighty-six per cent of entrepreneurs-turned-authors reported that their businesses had grown since launching their book.

But I couldn't write a book...

While all of this sounds great in theory, you're not a writer. You don't have the time. You're not even sure you know enough to fill a book. Could *you* really write a book?

Absolutely.

You don't need to be a professional writer. Of the many entrepreneurs I've worked with, only three of them had a writing background. (And those three books needed just as much reorganising and cutting as the non-writer books I've edited!)

My clients have come from a wide range of industries, including financial planning, accounting, travel, real estate, marketing, law, life coaching, human resources, natural health, personal training, business coaching, architecture, fashion and more. Writing experience is *not* a prerequisite to writing a great book. Planning and motivation are. If you have these, then you can write one too.

You also don't need a lot of time. We entrepreneurs are busy people. Between client work, quotes, enquiries, marketing and managing a team, it's not unusual to get to the end of the month and realise we haven't had a day off.[2]

Fortunately, writing a book doesn't have to take as long as you think. You don't need to spend months or years penning your masterpiece. Instead, if you have the right system in place, it will guide you through every step of the writing process so you never have to worry about running out of time, having writer's block or drawing a blank. With a system at your fingertips, you will have all the information you need to draft your book in weeks, not months.

But what if I fail?

So you're warming up to the idea of writing a book… at the very least, you can see some of the benefits it might have for your business. But what if you invest hundreds of hours, thousands of dollars and buckets of energy into writing a book, and it isn't any good? This is a concern I hear all the time.

If you've seen some of the books being self-published by entrepreneurs today, you might have noticed something. It's a thinly veiled fact that nobody dares mention…

---

2   To Andrew (my significant other) – I'm working on it!

Many books self-published by entrepreneurs aren't very good.[3]

Sure, the cover might look pretty swish and it feels satisfyingly heavy in your hands, but just wait until you get to the first page. Then Chapter 2. By Chapter 3, if you're like most people, you've probably given up.

Why?

Because the content wasn't credible, wasn't compelling or wasn't even coherent.

This isn't to say that the physical packaging of your book isn't important. It is. In fact, design is your first impression. But your content is the relationship, and if you want your book to lead to ongoing relationships with clients and partners it needs to be good.

So why do most entrepreneurs' words fail to live up to their covers?

I believe it comes down to a failure to plan.

A blueprint so detailed your book will write itself

Having worked as a professional writer and editor for the last eight years, and having worked with many entrepreneurs on their books since I launched my editing company, Grammar Factory, I've found that not having a detailed plan is the biggest mistake entrepreneurs make when writing their books.

Most people assume that an editor only looks at spelling, grammar and punctuation, but correcting language is

---

3   I wanted to say 'suck', but my editor wasn't a fan of that.

actually the smallest part of the job. The real work is in developing the idea, the structure and the content of the book. I've moved chapters from the middle of books to the beginning. I've turned three-part processes into six sequential steps. I've split one book into two, added brand new content, and told clients to start again.

Then what happens? The author receives a document marked up with a few thousand insertions, deletions, corrections, and suggestions to add new case studies, exercises and even chapters. And back to their keyboard they go.

Much of this could have been avoided if they'd started with a clear plan.

Now I know that planning isn't 'sexy'. As entrepreneurs we appreciate impulse, spontaneity, inspiration and leaps of faith. We don't have time for *planning*.

However, more often than not it's the books written on impulse with spontaneity as their muse that end up unfinished or forgotten in a file on a computer, or published but languishing in boxes in a garage, being eaten by cockroaches because no one wants to buy them.

These are the books that should have had a quarter of their content cut in the editing process because it's repetitive or irrelevant. They are the ones where the author's jumble of ideas should have been reworked into a logical, engaging structure.

In the worst-case scenario, they are the books where the author has to go back to the drawing board. Not very sexy, when you think about it.

So what *is* sexy?

Sexy is getting a box of 100 of your printed books and feeling confident, excited and proud about sending them out into the world. Sexy is when a reader calls or emails you to tell you how much they loved your book, and the difference it made to their life. Sexy is when a journalist runs a story on your industry and contacts you as an author to comment.

And sexy starts with planning.

What to expect from this book

This book is going to teach you how to write a book that will boost your business. The goal is that by the time you finish all of the exercises you will have a blueprint that's so detailed your book will write itself.

How do I know this?

This is the same formula I teach in book planning workshops. The strategies are the same ones I use to reorganise manuscripts and figure out what's missing. It's also the same process I used to write the book you have in your hands. And using this process, I finished my first draft in three days.

I'm not sharing this with you to brag.[4] I'm sharing this because what I've learnt after working with so many entrepreneurs on their books is that you don't need to be an experienced writer to write a great book. You don't need

---

4   Well, maybe a little.

to be inspired to find the right idea. You don't need to set aside months of your hard-earned time. All you need is the right formula, and to put your fingers to the keyboard.

So how do you do it? By addressing four key areas...

The right idea

What is the difference between entrepreneurs who push through the hurdles of writing and self-publishing and those who don't? How can some books from a particular industry be filled with practical, relevant and engaging content, while others from the same industry are filled with fluff, tangents and repetition? And why will readers pick up one book while ignoring another on the same topic?

It all comes down to choosing the right idea. In this section you'll figure out how to find an idea that hits the sweet spot, along with the right book type for that idea, which is the foundation for everything that follows.

The right structure

While most of my clients are genuinely experts in their fields and have the experience and qualifications to prove it, their books often need a lot of reworking to bring them to a publishable standard.

Why? Because the right idea won't stick if it isn't presented in a way that's clear, coherent and compelling. Likewise, the right content will fall flat (or will be missed entirely) if it isn't supported by a strong structure. Here you'll learn how to organise your knowledge, including the key questions that need to be answered in every chapter of your book.

The right content

While you might have a lot of great ideas, simply listing them in bullet-point form isn't enough to fill a book. To write a substantial piece of work, you need content.

By including explanations, evidence and exercises throughout your writing, you'll publish a book that is not only a credible representation of your business but one that will persuade your readers of your ideas and convince them to implement your advice.

The right language

A lot of entrepreneurs worry that there are already thousands of books out there on their area of expertise. I always counter with, 'You're the only *you* in your area of expertise.' And by being the only you, you can make your book stand out from all the others.

How do you do this? With your language. Your language is what will take your book from being a rambling diatribe written in dreary corporate speak to being a text that engages your readers and invites them to learn more about your business.

After addressing these four areas, you will have drafted a 3,000-to 5,000-word blueprint for your book.[5]

With this blueprint, you won't have to worry about writer's block, rambling, or forgetting key information. In fact, then the only thing you'll have to do is expand your bullet points into sentences, add a paragraph here and there, and drop in relevant blog posts and articles to flesh out your points.

In a matter of weeks, you can easily write a great book that will make you the authority you want to be.

Don't believe me?

Then keep reading.

---

5   This only counts if you do the worksheets and other actions throughout this book. If you don't do the worksheets, I can't guarantee anything. If you do all of the exercises and can't put a detailed plan together, I will happily refund your $24.95.

PART 1

THE RIGHT IDEA

CHAPTER 1

Hit the sweet spot

You might have been told that you have a book in you. I'm going to argue that you probably have seven or eight in you. As one of my clients once said, 'I've wanted to write books about managing change and building resilience and confidence, a book about careers, a book about life, a book about personal branding and professional image, and a book about dogs.'

The question isn't whether or not there's a book in you, it's whether it's the right book for right now. And writing the right book starts with choosing the right idea.

Not every idea is a great one. Not every idea will become a runaway success. In fact, very few book ideas make it to print. What you want to do is find the right idea at the beginning of the process, so you don't waste time, money and energy on any of the wrong ones.

So what makes a great book idea? Great book ideas reside at the intersection of these three elements:

- Your passion
- Your readers' needs
- Your knowledge

The mistake most entrepreneurs make is choosing an idea that only addresses *one* of these factors. This is a recipe for disaster. Your cake won't rise if you just put flour in it. It needs eggs, sugar and baking powder to make it fat, generous and delicious. The same goes for your book.

If you aren't passionate about your idea, you'll quickly run out of steam. Most entrepreneurs who fail the passion test give up partway through the writing process.

Meanwhile, those who do manage to push out 30,000 to 50,000 words often have nothing left to fuel them through the book production and marketing processes.

That said, it doesn't matter how passionate you are if you aren't addressing your readers' needs. For your book to build your business, boost your reputation and attract the opportunities that are only available to industry leaders, it needs to answer the wants and needs of your market. If it doesn't, no one will want to buy your book and you'll be left with a very expensive paperweight.

The final piece is knowledge. Many entrepreneurs are passionate. Many have a product or service or idea that their target clients desperately desire. However, not all of these products, services and ideas can be turned into a worthwhile book. There needs to be knowledge and content to back it up. If you don't have this knowledge, or access to it, you'll find yourself drawing a blank.

The right book at the right time is a book that hits the sweet spot – the intersection where these three factors meet.

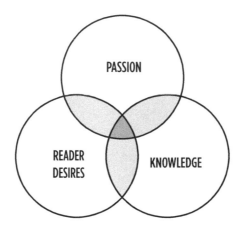

To find your sweet spot, you need to conduct three highly unscientific tests.

The passion test

I believe testing your passion for your idea comes down to answering one simple question:

Will you still want to talk about this in three years?

Why three years? Because it will probably take three years for your book to start bringing in real dividends, and your energy and commitment will be required to steer your book through those years. Surprised? Let me explain.

Let's say it takes you one month to write your book, squeezing in an hour or two a day around your existing commitments. Then you let your book sit for a couple of weeks before going back through it to see if there are any obvious gaps in your content, repetition or other issues.

Once you've completed your review, you send the manuscript to your editor. The first round of edits takes two weeks, after which you take the book back for a month to go through the recommended changes and add new content.

You then send it back to your editor so she can go through everything a second time and ensure the new content works with the rest of your book. This second edit takes another week or two.

While your book is being edited, you spend a month going back and forth with your cover designer to create a cover that stands out from the other books in your industry.

Next, a second designer or typesetter takes your edited content and creates the internal layout of your book. This may take another few weeks, depending on how much you love or hate their early ideas.

Once the layout is confirmed you organise printing. A printer will usually need a week or so to send you a proof copy, and after you approve it (or they make any requested changes) they will proceed with the full print run, which is another week or two.

Finally, you'll also need to organise online (Amazon, Book Depository, Booktopia and so on) and possibly offline (bookstores) distribution for your book.

All of this takes time, money and motivation. Even if you produce your book very quickly and cheaply, you're looking at a minimum of three months and probably $4,000 to $5,000. If you're like most people, you'll spend six to twelve months getting it right, and spend $5,000 to $10,000 on the production process.[6]

And this is only the production process – you aren't going to see a return on your investment unless you *market* your book, and you can expect to be marketing it for two to three years after it is printed.

Finding a topic you are passionate about is crucial – if you're already sick of your idea by the time your book goes to print, you aren't going to be interested in leveraging it, which can turn this 'writing a book thing' into a very expensive exercise.

Action time – What would you love to write about?

Take five minutes to reflect on what you would love to write a book about. Which topics excite you? What can you talk about for hours?

Think about why you originally started your business (or why you're thinking about starting a business). What is the purpose or message behind it? What do you love about what you do?

Make a list of your different book ideas. Then, for each of them, ask yourself, 'Will I still want to talk about this in three years?'

If not, cross it off. The remaining ideas are your shortlist.

---

6   These prices and timeframes are based on the Australian self-publishing industry. Self-publishing in the US, the UK and other countries may vary.

The reader test

Your passion will fuel you through the writing, production and marketing processes. But what use is that fuel if no one wants to read the end result?

Your book will only be an effective marketing tool if people want to read it. And making people want to read your book usually means you have to do one of two things: solve a thorny problem, or meet a burning desire.

If you get this bit right, this will be the pull factor that not only gets you readers but leads to new clients, media attention and speaking opportunities.

So what is the reader test? This time there are three questions:

1. Who are your target readers?

2. What are their greatest problems and desires?

3. What are you *really* writing about?

Let's take a look at each of these questions.

1. Who are your target readers?

As an entrepreneur, your target readers will probably be drawn from one of three groups: potential clients, potential partners or the media.

In some cases, you might find that these groups can be broken down further. If we consider potential clients, for example, a dance teacher might be able to target parents who want their children to start ballet as well as dance teachers who want to become accredited in her teaching methodology. A risk management software provider could target the end users as well as the companies he wants to install the software. A road safety school could target students, as well as those tasked with enforcing road rules.

Regardless of your situation and your business, you can only choose *one* audience for your book. The dance teacher might choose parents who want their children to be more active, the software developer might target companies, and the road safety trainer might focus on potential students. By choosing these audiences, they have chosen *not* to write for their other potential audiences.

Now, I can hear you saying, 'But I want *all* of those people to read my book.'

Of course there's no reason why you can't *leverage* your book for all of these audiences, but when it comes to *writing* your book, you need to have one primary audience. Committing to this one audience gives your writing direction. If you know what that audience cares about, you will know which topics to include, and which topics to cut. You'll know which examples will most resonate, and which would be better discussed in another format, like a blog post or brochure. You'll also know which action steps and exercises are most relevant.

On the other hand, if you try to write for everyone your book will lack focus. Some content will be relevant to everyone, while other content will only be relevant to a single audience. You might even find that you write your book predominantly for one audience, only to throw in an extra chapter or two for the secondary audience you wanted to target. The risk is that when your readers come across content that doesn't relate to them, they will put your book down, never to open it again.

So who do you choose? The answer is, the audience that is most likely to have the biggest, fastest impact on your business.

Let's repeat that: You want to write for the audience that is *most likely to* have the *biggest, fastest* impact on your business.

In most cases, that is not the media. Yes, the media could have a big impact on your business. And, if your story catches on, it could spiral very quickly. But the first thing to consider is whether this is likely. Given the number of other books out there, and the fact that most news stories go out of date within a couple of days (or within a few hours, in today's twenty-four-hour news cycle), it probably isn't.

Additionally, while media attention could lead to more eyes on your business, it's unlikely that the reporters themselves will actually become paying clients. As a result, there's no guarantee that a book targeted at the media will lead to increased revenue.

Instead, the readers most likely to have a significant impact on your business are your potential clients. If you write a book that addresses their greatest problems and most burning desires, they will probably keep reading. They will probably go to your website to learn more about you. They will probably refer you to other people they know with the same problems and desires. And they will be more likely to choose to work with you than the media ever will.

This doesn't mean you will miss out on partnerships or media opportunities. Instead, when it comes to approaching potential partners and journalists, you can use your book as a credibility tool by highlighting the fact that you're a published author, rather than trying to repurpose your content for a new audience. This means the people who are most likely to read the book get bespoke content, while those who are not in your primary market can still confidently work with you knowing that you are an established expert.

So who are your target readers?

Action time – Who are your target readers?

Is your book for potential clients, potential partners, or the media?

Once you know which category your target readers fall into, the next step is adding more detail.

Think about:

- Their age and gender
- Their marital status and children
- Where they live
- Their occupation/business and their income
- What they do in their free time
- What they value/believe
- What they read, watch and listen to (books, magazines, online, TV, radio)

An area where a lot of my clients get stuck is trying to define clear boundaries for each of these questions. For example, if you're a psychologist who has been practising for twenty years, you might know that people come to see you because they've become disillusioned with life and don't know what to do about it. However, those people might be aged anywhere between twenty-five and sixty-five, they might be single or married, they might be male or female, and they might work in a range of industries. In this case it's easy to wonder how to define your target readers when they come from all walks of life.

To define your target readers, it's important to get as specific as possible in the areas that are relevant to your business. Depending on your target reader and your business, some of the areas listed in the previous exercise might not be relevant. For example, my team and I have worked with entrepreneurs who have written books on financial planning, entrepreneurship, property investing, health and wellness, immigration, personal development, and even one on travelling with your pet! As these clients aren't restricted to a single industry, I didn't target this book at any one industry.

The key is to focus on the attributes your target readers share. In our case, even though our clients come from a range of industries, they share the traits of entrepreneurship, a focus on delivering high-quality work and the desire to become industry leaders.

In short, when defining your target readers, don't be put off by broad differences between them. Instead, look for patterns and commonalities. You'd be surprised at how people from different walks of life can have a similar problem or ambition. Which brings us to the second question...

2. What are their problems and desires?

Once you know your target readers, the next step is to figure out their thorniest problems and most burning desires. These problems and desires should be the foundation of your book idea and, if you use these well, you'll write a book that they'll be dying to read.

As an entrepreneur, you know that the purpose of your business is to solve people's problems. As an entrepreneur writing a book, your book has the same purpose.

By targeting your readers' biggest problems and desires, your book will bring a flood of highly targeted opportunities to your business. Whether you're pitching to a new client, a partner or a journalist, the sale will be easier as the person you're speaking to will be pre-sold. And easier sales means more money, which means you can further expand your business.

Keep in mind that the problems and desires you address in your book will change based on your target reader. If your target reader is a potential client, you would base your book on the most common problems and desires you see in your existing clients. So if you are a real estate agent and your book is about property investment, your readers' biggest problems or fears might include buying the wrong property, choosing the wrong tenant and hiring the wrong property manager, all of which could turn their investment into a headache that might lose them money. Your readers' most burning desire might be to generate stress-free passive income. In this case, your book would teach them how to achieve that goal while avoiding the problems that prevent most would-be property investors from doing so.

If your book was targeted at potential partners, however, the focus would be completely different. To use the real estate agent example again, you might want to establish a community collective between a real estate agent and a group of trades to act as a one-stop-shop for your tenants and landlords should an issue arise. As your readers are now the group of trades, and any other potential partners, the main problems might be struggling to stand out in a crowded marketplace, customers shopping around for the best rate, and not knowing how to extend their reach. Their ultimate desire might be to have regular, reliable business coming in without having to worry about marketing. In this case, your book might be about the power of partnerships to boost small businesses.

If you wanted to target the media, you would need to revisit the problems and desires of journalists and media personalities. As a general rule, the main problem any journalist faces is coming up with a great story, and their greatest desire is to find one. The challenge for you is providing that story. As a real estate agent, it might be something about the property price bubble, such as touching on some sort of conspiracy behind it or warning about an eventual pop.

Action time – Pain points and burning desires

What are your target readers' biggest problems? What would they pay anything to solve?

Think about:

- What do they fear?
- What frustrates them?
- What causes them the most stress?

Then, think about their greatest desires:

- What do they want?
- What are they really trying to get done?

Revisit your book ideas. Which of these subjects address the questions above? Or, based on these questions, are there new ideas you can add to the list?

What do you do if you have a book idea, and you know it's an important problem for your readers to solve, but you don't think they realise that it's a problem?

Here you have two options: you can either go back to the drawing board to find a new idea, or you can stick with your existing one. The challenge with sticking with the existing idea is that you will need to work much harder to sell it to your readers.

In early 2014 I worked with a photographer who had written a book about helping people organise and store their digital photos. Now this book answers the real problem of potentially losing all of your precious photos because you haven't stored them properly. The issue with this idea is that it is a preventative solution – a solution to prevent a problem from occurring – rather than a solution to a problem the readers are already facing. The issue with preventative solutions is that there's no sense of urgency. The problem is abstract. And this means solving it isn't compelling. It's only *after* the problem has occurred – *after* someone has lost all of their photos – that they see the importance of creating a system to organise and back up their images.

So what did we do? We focused on selling his readers on the importance of solving this problem upfront by starting the book with a story about a friend who embarked on a long-awaited trip to Cambodia. She visited temples, rice terraces and landscapes, and at the end of each day she sat back with a glass of wine and sifted through the day's photos. When she returned home, she narrowed her collection of several thousand snaps down to the 300 best images, which she painstakingly tweaked and refined before saving them to an external hard drive. A few days later she reconnected the hard drive to view her holiday snaps ... but the photos were gone.

By telling this story at the beginning, we were able to make readers imagine what would happen if *they* lost everything, which made the rest of the book more compelling.

If you're writing about a real problem, but not one that your ideal clients recognise, think about how you can convince them of the importance of this problem before you teach them how to solve it.

3. What are you really writing about?

In 1960, Theodore Levitt published an article in the *Harvard Business Review* titled 'Marketing Myopia', where he argued that one of the reasons businesses fall into decline is that they don't understand the business they are really in.

'The railroads did not stop growing because the need for passenger and freight transportation declined. That grew. The railroads are in trouble today not because that need was filled by others (cars, trucks, airplanes, and even telephones) but because it was *not* filled by the railroads themselves. They let others take customers away from them because they assumed themselves to be in the railroad business rather than in the transportation business. The reason they defined their industry incorrectly was that they were railroad oriented instead of transportation oriented; they were product oriented instead of customer oriented.'[7]

Finding the right answer to the question, 'What business are you really in?' gives your business the ability to evolve with the industry landscape and to continue serving your clients what they desire. This makes it the key to your business's long-term survival.

I could make the same argument about your book.

Most books by entrepreneurs aren't just about money management or weight loss or property acquisition. They

---

7   Theodore Levitt, 'Marketing Myopia', *Harvard Business Review*, August 2004, Accessed November 23, 2014. https://hbr.org/2004/07/marketing-myopi

are about being able to sleep at night, confidence and vitality, and financial freedom. Angela Counsel, author of *Secret Mums' Business*, didn't write a book about how her readers could eat better, exercise more or improve their mindset; she wrote about how mums could find more balance and fulfilment in their lives. Warren Otter, author of *Crank it UP*, didn't write a book about mergers and acquisitions; he wrote about how entrepreneurs could leave a legacy through their businesses.

The photographer I mentioned earlier didn't write a book about organising digital photos. He wrote a book about protecting digital memories.

Action time – What are you really writing about?

What is the result you want your readers to achieve through reading your book? If you could summarise that in twenty words or less, what would it be?

This is what you're *really* writing about. Once you nail this phrase, it will become how you pitch your book once it's published, and it may even become part of your title or subtitle.

Once again, revisit your list of book ideas. Which ones focus on the business you're *really* in?

Take it to your target readers

So far this has all been academic – you've been thinking about what you *think* your readers want. The real test is taking it to your target readers to learn about what they *actually* want.

Action time – Test your idea

Test your idea on your target readers. If you already know people who fit your target reader profile, try the following:

- Call them up or take them out to coffee to pitch your idea.

- Write some blog posts about your idea to see how they respond.

- Tweak your products and services to incorporate your book idea and observe the difference it makes.

The knowledge test

Have you ever read a book that promised great things – to teach you a new skill, to solve a niggling issue, or to help you reach your dreams – that failed to deliver? It's almost like getting a massage where the masseuse misses all of the right spots: frustrating, unfulfilling and likely to leave you more wound up than you were at the beginning of the massage. You're also unlikely to go back a second time. If you promise to solve your readers' burning issues or help them achieve their desires and your book doesn't deliver, your readers are also likely to finish your book feeling frustrated and unfulfilled – if they finish it at all. They probably aren't going to subscribe to your newsletter, follow you on social media or engage your services either.[8]

So, the final test to find the right book idea is the knowledge test. Maybe you are just starting out in a new field and you're writing a book in an effort to establish yourself, or maybe you've been in your industry for years but you're still not *quite* sure you know enough to fill a book. In either case, it doesn't matter how passionate you are about a topic or how much your target readers want to learn about it if you don't have the knowledge to back it up.

A question that often comes up at this point is, 'Can't I just research my subject?' If you're passionate about your idea, it's easy to believe that you'll do the research required to fill your knowledge gaps. You'll Google, read, enrol in a course and more. While this is an option, there are two issues with taking this approach.

The first is that you need a certain level of knowledge to guide your research. Let's consider my gardening abilities for a moment. I have none. In fact, I don't even have a garden – my partner and I have a deck that features some potted herbs. Unfortunately, none of these herbs lasts long. Our thyme was cannibalised by our oregano. The oregano then shrivelled up (I assume it was starved of nutrients). Our basil plant shed all its leaves. And our mint spends weeks looking like it's dead, only

---

8   This is known as negative marketing.

to spring back to life the week before we were planning to rip it out.[9] Now if I decided to write a book about raising healthy avocado trees, I wouldn't know where to start. I might turn to Google with a generic search about growing avocado trees, but this search would only return generic advice. Why? Because I don't know the right questions to ask.

By contrast, an avocado farmer already has a system he uses for his trees. This means he knows what works and what doesn't, he knows how to filter the useless advice from the helpful advice, and he probably knows the common issues and questions that come up for new gardeners raising their first avocado tree.

Consequently, he can ask specific questions to guide his research. He also has access to much more qualified resources, such as his fellow avocado farmers, whom he can contact for targeted advice.

While your passion is the fuel that keeps you going, your knowledge is your road map. If you don't have knowledge to guide you, your journey to writing a book will be a directionless ramble.

The second issue with using research to build your knowledge is that, while it's very rewarding to immerse yourself in a new topic, it does take time to reach expert status. The more time you spend researching, the longer you put off actually writing and leveraging your book for your business. And if you're like most of my authors, you want to get your book done as efficiently as possible so you can start leveraging it sooner rather than later.

---

9   Yet somehow our weeds thrive...

So how do you know if you have enough knowledge about your book idea? Simply follow the exercises in this book. As you map out your structure in Part 2 and choose the content to fill that structure in Part 3, you will find yourself describing your idea in increasing levels of detail. Starting with an overarching idea for your book, you will break that idea into smaller topics, and break each of those topics into smaller subtopics. For every single one of these topics, you'll need to answer various questions to cover them in depth and collect evidence to illustrate your points.

Whether or not you can answer these questions and can find this evidence will be the true test of your knowledge.

For now, though, here's one technique you can use to get started…

Map it out

One of the best techniques for getting your ideas on paper, especially if you're not a writer, is mind mapping.

A mind map is a diagram you can use to record and organise your ideas, and they have been used by some of the greatest minds of the last five hundred years, including Leonardo da Vinci, Charles Darwin, Albert Einstein, Thomas Edison, Winston Churchill, Pablo Picasso and more. And, over the past thirty years, dozens of studies have found that mind maps are an excellent tool for improving memory, generating ideas and organising those ideas, which makes them extremely useful for new authors.

A 2009 paper on how using mind mapping software might improve freshman students' writing skills found that mind mapping software improved students' ability to both generate ideas and organise them more effectively, as the spatial layout helped students gain a better overview of a subject and made connections between topics more visible. This then triggered more thoughts, ideas and associations.[10]

Meanwhile, a 2002 study that measured the effectiveness of student nurses using mind maps to plan patient care found that student nurses who used mind maps had a greater ability to focus on the patient, make connections between symptoms, see the big picture, and be more creative when providing treatments.

If you apply these findings to your book, you could argue that mind mapping will give you a greater ability to stay focused on your target reader, make connections between various topics, keep everything connected to the major problem or desire you're addressing, and come up with more creative solutions and recommendations.[11]

Finally, if you don't consider yourself to be a natural writer, you'll be pleased to discover that mind maps are also a powerful tool for improving your writing. The

10   Reima Al-Jarf, 'Enhancing Freshman students' Writing Skills with a Mind Mapping software', Paper presented at the 5th International Scientific Conference, eLearning and Software for Education, Bucharest, April 2009.

11   Mueller, A, Johnston, M and Bligh, D, 'Joining Mind Mapping and Care Planning to Enhance Student Critical Thinking and Achieve Holistic Nursing Care', *Nursing Diagnosis* (2002), 24.

study I mentioned earlier on freshman writing skills and mind mapping software found that the work produced by students using mind maps included more relevant detail, and that their ideas were both better organised and more clearly connected than the ideas of those who didn't use mind maps.[12]

In short, by quickly getting your key ideas on paper, seeing the relationships between them and being able to organise them in meaningful ways, the writing process becomes easier and quicker. And mind maps are a key way to achieve this.

So why are they so effective?

A mind map is structured with a central idea in the middle of the page, smaller ideas surrounding it, and subtopics of those smaller ideas surrounding them. This is known as a radiant structure. Unlike the linear structure of lists and tables, the radiant structure of mind maps mimics the natural function of our brains.[13] This allows you to see connections and relationships that wouldn't be as obvious in linear lists, which then triggers more related ideas and enables you to organise these ideas more easily.

By combining this radiant structure with the use of symbols, images and colour as well as words, you access your right brain as well as your left brain, which further enhances your ability to process information, make connections and generate ideas.

---

12   Reima Al-Jarf, 'Enhancing Freshman students' Writing Skills with a Mind Mapping software', Paper presented at the 5th International Scientific Conference, eLearning and Software for Education, Bucharest, April 2009.

13   Petr Anokhin, 'The forming of natural and artificial intelligence', *Impact of Science in Society* (1973), Vol. XXIII 3.

As a result, the most effective way to test your knowledge is to map out your book idea.

Action time – Map out your idea

Review your book idea shortlist – these are the ideas that pass both the passion test and the reader test. Choose one and map it out, following the steps below.

1. Get a large piece of butcher's paper or poster paper and turn it sideways.

2. Write down a couple of key words that represent your idea in the middle of the page.

3. Write down any related ideas you can think of, drawing curved branches from your central idea to each of the related ideas.

4. Look at each of the second-level ideas. Can you think of any ideas that relate to those second-level ideas? Write them down, connecting them to the second-level ideas with more branches.

5. Once you run out of steam, review your second- and third-level ideas. For each idea, think about any existing content you have, research you've been doing, or clients you've worked with. Also consider any research you'd like to do for that idea. Make a note of each of these next to the relevant idea, connecting them with more branches.

Things to keep in mind as you do this exercise:

- Try to incorporate colours and images to help your brain make more associations.

- Use curved branches rather than straight ones – according to Tony Buzan, the father of modern mind mapping, curved lines are more likely to engage your brain.[14]

- Focus on high-level ideas for now – you will go into more detail in Part 2.

- Don't worry too much about grouping or organising any of your scribbles – we'll start doing that in Part 2. This is just a brain dump so you can start to assess whether you could actually write a book on your topic.

Choosing your book idea

If you have a number of ideas on your shortlist, map out each of them to figure out which one generates the most related ideas. You can then use that idea for the rest of the exercises in this book. Don't worry about whether or not you're committing to the right idea – the purpose of this chapter is to find an idea that hits the idea sweet spot, which you can then use to work through the rest of this book. Even if you change your

---

14   Buzan, T and Buzan, B (1994), *The Mind Map Book: How to use radiant thinking to maximize your brain's untapped potential.* Dutton.

mind later, you'll still have the framework to write an awesome book on another idea.

If you only have one idea on your shortlist, how do you know if you've passed the knowledge test? As a guide, if you struggle to think of related subtopics for your idea, if you can't think of anything new after five minutes, or if you struggle to fill the page, you might not have enough to write about. However, if you find yourself running out of room on the page, or every note you write sparks a new idea about something to look up or someone to call, then you've passed the knowledge test and hit the sweet spot.

The next step is choosing the right book type.

CHAPTER 2

The right book type for your idea

Now you've found an idea that hits the sweet spot. But how do you turn that idea into a book? The next step is choosing a book type.

Great books come in all shapes and sizes, and entrepreneurs usually write one of the following:

1. The how-to book
2. The thought leadership book
3. The list book
4. The interview book
5. The memoir

Depending on your idea, any one of these might be an option. If you are a life coach specialising in helping women with their self-esteem, for example, your how-to book might be your seven-step process to help women improve their self-esteem. A thought leadership book in this area might discuss why self-esteem is so important for women today. A list book could be *365 Tips to Boost Your Self-esteem*, where your readers could have one tip for every day of the year. An interview book might feature interviews from five prominent women in business or the arts and cover their journeys to find self-love. A memoir, on the other hand, would be about your own journey to improve your self-esteem.

While all of these can work well, the mistake many entrepreneurs make is writing without choosing a single book type. They write about their story, add five chapters that cover five steps, add some interviews, and hope for the best.

When it comes to editing, this will either result in a very confused editor who doesn't know what you want to achieve and so only does a proofread rather than reviewing your content and structure, or an editor who edits your book to fit one of the five book types, resulting in any content that isn't relevant to that book type being cut.[15] And, if you change your mind afterwards, that means you need to write more new content and go through another round of editing.

Each of these book types works differently. Each has a different structure, each includes different content, and each uses different language. The swiftest route to success is to choose a book type at the beginning, and write within its conventions.

So which is right for you?

---

15   We had one case where a client's word count dropped by over fifty per cent.

1. The how-to book

Often structured as X steps to achieve a certain result, in a how-to book you teach your readers how to solve a problem or achieve a goal using your unique process. If you own a service-based business and personally work with clients or groups, this will probably be a good choice as you will already have a process you take your clients through.

These books have a practical focus, with exercises, thinking questions and action steps for each piece of advice the author gives. As there's a clear way to get value from your book, these books are very appealing to readers – all they need to do is follow your steps.

From a writer's perspective, how-to books are also a great way to get started because they are very formulaic. As a result, once you learn the formula, all you need to do is add your knowledge and you'll have a great book on your hands.[16]

But what if you don't have a process? Many entrepreneurs in service-based businesses get stuck at this point, because they feel like their work is highly tailored to each client. If this is you, you might be surprised. Even if each of your clients is unique, they will share common traits. After all, those traits are why they all chose to work with you!

The trick is to focus on the common traits – rather than what makes them different – and the stages you usually take your clients through in your work together.

---

16   You'll learn more about this formula in Part 2.

For example, some things that often come up, regardless of industry, include:

- An assessment stage, or 'where are you now?',

- A goal-setting stage, or 'where do you want to be?',

- Mapping out the steps from their current state to their goal,

- Engaging a team to help with the process,

- Measuring their success, and

- Next steps after they achieve their goal.

Another approach is looking at the key areas you need to cover, rather than trying to put things into a step-by-step process. That's what I've done with this book.

While every book is different, the four areas I look at for every book are the idea, the structure, the content and the language. When I realised this, these four areas became the framework for this book.

Action time – Your how-to mind map

Take out another piece of butcher's paper or poster paper and write your book idea in the centre of the page in a how-to phrase. For example, you might write 'how to do/achieve/ learn [insert your subject].'

Then map out the process you take your clients through, making each step or area you cover a second-level idea. Rather than looking at what makes each client unique, think about the common threads: what are the common areas you look at, the common stages you go through, or the common hurdles you help them avoid?

Once you have a handful of steps (five to nine usually works well, however focus on what you need to cover to get the result your clients want), think about subtopics for each of those steps. In each stage of your process, what do your clients need to know? What do they need to do?

2. The thought leadership book

The second type of book for entrepreneurs is the thought leadership book.

Rather than taking readers through a process to achieve a result, thought leadership books are more persuasive, focusing on making your case for something you believe in. This can work well for entrepreneurs who:

- Have a highly customised process that can't easily be broken into steps,

- Have a highly involved process with many steps that occur at the same time, making them difficult to explain in sequence (this often happens with very large corporate projects), or

- Work in a field that isn't widely understood or accepted.

Because you aren't offering a lot of practical advice, these books focus on explaining a theory or philosophy, linking this to the problems your readers are experiencing and describing how your theory can solve them, using examples, case studies, industry studies and statistics as evidence.

One excellent example of this type of book is Lissa Rankin's *Mind over Medicine*, which makes the case for the power of the mind to heal our bodies, and shares various studies that validate her theory.

When done well, thought leadership books can be very powerful and are far more likely to start movements than how-to books. However, they require a very clear contention and a lot of research to get right.

Action time – Your thought leadership mind map

Take out another piece of butcher's paper or poster paper and write your book idea in the centre of the page in a thought leadership phrase. For example, you might write 'why [insert your topic] is important for [your readers].'

Then map out the reasons why this is so important, making each topic a second-level idea. These ideas might include benefits your readers will experience when they address your topic, problems if they don't, different areas of their lives it may affect, and more.

Once you have exhausted your reasons for why your topic is important, focus on each of your second-level ideas. What research, case studies, academic studies, statistics, interviews and more do you have to back up your claims? Write them down.

3. The list book

The list book is a list of tips and tricks to help your readers solve a problem or achieve a goal. While the purpose is similar to a how-to book, the difference is that the advice in a list book doesn't need to be followed in order. While a seven-step process in a how-to book needs to be read (and implemented) sequentially for your readers to achieve the best results, the goal with a list book is for your readers to be able to open it on any page and receive some valuable advice.

So how many tips do you need to fill a list book? It depends on your idea, how detailed your tips are and how long you want your book to be. In an A4 document, a 30,000-word draft is usually between seventy and eighty pages and each page is between 400 and 500 words. If each tip is one page, or about 500 words, then you'd be looking at between fifty and sixty tips. (Keep in mind that you'll also need some pages for your introduction and conclusion.) If each tip is half an A4 page, or 250 words, you'll need 100 to 120 tips.

If you have fewer than ten pieces of advice, focus on fleshing each of those out in detail and writing a how-to book instead of a list book.

Action time – Your list book mind map

Once again, take out a new piece of poster paper. Or, if you struggled to flesh out the ideas in the how-to mind map you created earlier, revisit that one.

What are all the little pieces of advice someone needs to know about your topic? What are the common questions your clients ask you? What are the questions they *should* ask you, but don't? What are the common mistakes they make?

Don't worry if you can't discuss all of these points in detail – if you have enough of them, one page will be plenty. For now, just jot down key words for each of them as second-level topics.

Then look over what you've done. Do you have enough separate points to create a list book? Ideally, you want more than fifty separate tips.

4. The interview book

The bulk of the content in this type of book comes from interviews. (A related book type is one in which a number of different experts submit a chapter.)

I feel like a lot of entrepreneurs see the interview book as an easy way out. If other experts are providing most of your content, there's less for you to do! Right?

In theory, yes. However, most interview books, or books with chapters written by different experts, simply aren't very good books.

The first issue with interview books, or books with multiple contributors, is that they can very easily turn into mediocre books. As soon as you put your book into someone else's hands, you lose control over the quality of the content, and it can be difficult to ask someone to redo their work if they're giving you content as a favour, or if they've paid to be a part of your book.

The second issue is that publishing a book that collates a collection of other experts' viewpoints will dilute the power of your book to build your reputation as an expert in your field. An interview book doesn't share your knowledge, ideas, advice or research – the entire book is based on *other people's* knowledge, ideas, advice and research.

The third issue is that, unless you're very clear from the beginning about a common theme, story or message that will tie all of the separate interviews or contributions together, your book can feel like a collection of articles rather than a cohesive piece of work. This creates an unfulfilling experience for your readers, making them less likely to read the entire book. After all, if you're not taking them on a journey from one interview to the next, why should they keep reading?

If you do have a clear story you want to tell and your interviewees or contributors are happy to let you have full editorial control, then this book type can work well.

One example of an interview book done well is Monique Bayer's *Devouring Melbourne*. Monique Bayer's company, Walk Melbourne, does foodie walking tours of Melbourne, and *Devouring Melbourne* is about celebrating some of the food secrets she uncovers on these tours. While the bulk of the content comes from interviews with the owners of the establishments she frequents, it's all tied together with the history of the different cuisines you'll find in Melbourne.

Action time – Your interview book mind map

You guessed it – time for another mind map! If you already know that a how-to, thought leadership or list book isn't right for you, would an interview book be an option?

Take out another piece of poster paper, and in the centre write 'interviews that share/demonstrate [key message] about [your topic]'. Remember, the message that links these interviews is just as important as the interviews themselves.

Now think about who you could interview about your topic. Who would have something to contribute to your key message? Whose story is a clear example of the message you want to share? Write them down.

5. The memoir

The memoir sounds pretty self-explanatory – it's just you telling your story… isn't it? Yes, it is telling your story, but the challenge is doing this in a way that will make people want to read it. In other words, your memoir needs to pass the reader test. Most self-published memoirs don't.

If you look at the memoirs that are most successful, they typically have one of the following attributes:

- They tell an extraordinary story,

- They are tied together by a key message or lesson, or

- They tell the story of someone who has already achieved fame and success.

These three attributes pass the reader test. In the case of an extraordinary story, they satisfy the reader's desire to escape from their everyday life, to be moved and to be inspired, much like when reading a fictional story.

In the case of the memoir that teaches a lesson or shares a message, they satisfy the reader's desire to reflect on their own lives in the context of that lesson or message.

In the case of the person who is already famous or successful, these memoirs satisfy the reader's desire to learn more about someone they admire, to discover how they achieved their success, and, once again, to be inspired.

Unfortunately, very few of the self-published memoirs out there tell extraordinary stories. How many of us survived Nazi concentration camps? How many of us have learnt to walk again after being paralysed? How many of us have successfully launched global charities? Not many.

Additionally, very few self-published memoirs are tied together by a strong theme or lesson. Instead, most read like a chronological list of events ('this happened and then this happened…').

Finally, most self-published memoirs aren't written by those who have already achieved fame or success. After all, if you're Mark Zuckerberg or Richard Branson, why would you need to self-publish your memoir? You'd have major publishers knocking down your door!

If you are considering writing a memoir, think about:

- Do you actually have an extraordinary story to tell? Did you learn to walk again after being paralysed? Did you escape from a cult?

- Will your readers learn an important lesson from your story?

- Are you already Mark Zuckerberg or Richard Branson, with publishers bidding on your unpublished story?

If not, I wouldn't recommend writing a memoir, particularly not for your first book.

This doesn't mean that your story doesn't have value, or that it hasn't contributed to the wisdom you want to share in your book. I'm sure it has. However, that doesn't mean it's memoir material.

So does that mean you can't share your story at all? Quite the contrary. Sharing your story in a how-to book, thought leadership book or list book has a number of benefits. First, an overview of how you achieved your present-day success and knowledge is a great way to build your credibility in your introduction. Second, sharing personal anecdotes throughout your book helps your readers get to know you. This makes you more personable and memorable as an author, and the readers who are drawn to your personality will be more likely to turn into paying clients. Third, examples of lessons you've learnt and mistakes you've made can be used as evidence to illustrate key points throughout the book.

And then, once you become a bestselling author, you'll be able to claim your place on the pedestal next to Zuckerberg and Branson, and write your memoir as book number two!

Action time – Your memoir mind map

Determined to tell your story? Then take out another piece of butcher's paper and start mapping it out.

I recommend focusing on the core message or lesson you want to share, and then noting the stories and anecdotes that help illustrate that message. Notice if a certain period of your life keeps coming up – could that form the basis of this book?

Finally, think about your readers. Will they want to read this? Will it add value to them? Will they learn an important lesson? Will they feel inspired? Serving your reader is the key to hitting the sweet spot.

Which book type is right for you?

Now that you know the five book types for entrepreneurs, which should you choose?

After doing the exercises in this chapter, you will probably find that there are already one or two book types you are gravitating toward. These are the book types where completing the mind map was easy – you had several broad ideas relating to your subject, and each of those ideas sparked smaller related ideas. If this is you then congratulations – you can focus on this book type as you work through this book and create your blueprint.

If you still aren't sure, that's okay – I'll be delving into these book types in more detail in Chapter 4, which will give you the opportunity to continue building on your mind maps to figure out the book type that's right for you. As a general guide, most entrepreneurs start with how-to, thought leadership and list books, which will be my focus as we start to explore chapter structure and content in Parts 2 and 3.

Bonus resource

Feeling a bit theoretical? Get instant access to the different mind maps I created for this book at grammarfactory.com/bb-bonus

IDEA WORKSHEET

1. Write down your book idea in one sentence.

2. Will you still want to talk about this subject in three years? If not, go back to the drawing board.

3. Who are your target readers?

    *   Is your book for potential clients, potential partners, or the media?

    *   What are their biggest problems and greatest desires?

    *   How will your book solve these problems or help them attain these desires?

4. Test your idea on your target readers. If you already know people who fit your target reader profile, try the following:

    *   Call them up or take them out to coffee to pitch your idea.

    *   Write some blog posts or an eBook about your idea to see how they respond.

    *   Tweak your products and services to incorporate your book idea and observe the difference it makes.

5. Once you're happy your idea passes the passion test and the reader test, brainstorm your book idea with a mind map:

- Get a large piece of butcher's paper or poster paper.

- Write your idea in the middle of the page.

- Write down any related ideas you can think of, drawing branches from your central idea to the related ideas.

- Look at each of the related ideas, and think about the ideas that are related to those smaller ideas.

- Think about any existing content you have, research you've been doing, or clients you've worked with. Make a note of these next to any relevant ideas on the page.

6. Choose your book type:

- Imagine how your book idea would work as a how-to book, a thought leadership book, a list book, an interview book or a memoir. Which type would best suit your idea?

- Once you've chosen your book type, create a new mind map with that focus – a how-to book on your industry would be very different to a memoir.

- If you aren't sure which book type will work for you, do a mind map for each of them to see where you have the most knowledge to share.

PART 2

THE RIGHT STRUCTURE

CHAPTER 3

Think content is king? Think again

When was the last time you picked up a business book and couldn't figure out what the author was talking about? Sure, the title sounded great, and they had the qualifications, but they kept jumping from topic to topic without any concrete advice to support their arguments (or if there *was* concrete advice, you missed it).

Your content is important – no argument here. After all, it doesn't matter how much style you have if there's no substance. However, for your content to have any impact it needs to be delivered in an easily digestible form. You create this with your structure.

The mistake most entrepreneurs make is that they have no clear structure when they start their books. Instead they take their idea, do some brainstorming, and then launch into the writing process.

And that's where the problems start. At Grammar Factory, seventy-five per cent of our clients lose over 7,000 words in their first round of edits. Most end up with a completely different structure. And occasionally we advise clients to write a new book.

Why? Because they didn't organise their thoughts before writing.

By contrast, creating a clear structure upfront will ensure your readers will love you, you'll boost your credibility *and* you'll sail through the writing process.

Readers love structure

Imagine pitching a solution to a client. You've been working for weeks on this proposal. You've analysed their problems, tailored a solution, and know it can deliver real benefits. From your perspective, this job could open up more opportunities for large-scale projects with similar clients.

You start to talk. You outline the products you want to use, the processes you'll follow and the technical specifications. You explain all of the benefits these changes will have for the client. You find yourself getting more and more excited as you think, 'This is in the bag. There's no way they can say no now.'

But then you notice their eyes have glazed over. They stifle a yawn and play with their phone under the table. While you were lost in your grand visions and hypothetical meanderings, they were just lost. And you have no idea how to get them back.

Now imagine trying to make the same pitch via the written page, where you have no body language, eye contact, intonation or conversational back-and-forth to keep things on track. Are things more likely to run off course? Absolutely.

While you might understand everything that's going on in your head, your readers don't. They don't have your years of experience and expertise. They don't always understand how you make the mental leap from one idea to the next. While you recognise something is important, they might not. This means you need to hold their hand as you take them through concepts and processes that are second nature to you.

You can't do this without a clear structure. If you write without a clear structure you're likely to just start typing everything that comes to mind, which will have no logical flow to an outsider. And if it has no logical flow to your readers, they aren't going to keep reading, they aren't going to be sold on your products and services, and your book isn't going to translate into new business.

On the other hand, writing with a clear structure makes your book easier to read. It means your readers are more likely to understand what you do and how it can benefit them, and – in the case of a how-to book – it means they're more likely to put the techniques you recommend into practice. Consequently, your readers are more likely to experience real-world benefits, and when your readers experience real-world benefits this means more good reviews for you and that your book gets recommended to more readers and potential clients.

Structure creates credibility

I know you know your stuff. If you didn't, you wouldn't even be considering writing a book. However, writing a book with no clear structure can be more detrimental to your credibility than not having a book at all.

Why? Because most of us subconsciously believe that the way you do one thing is the way you do everything. If your book is chaotic and disorganised, this means your readers will connect those qualities to your business.

And this doesn't just go for readers who are potential clients – what about those who are potential partners? If you can't structure your book well, do you really think a partner will have faith in your ability to structure a proposal? Do you think an event coordinator will believe you can deliver a compelling keynote presentation? The only indication the event coordinator has of how you'll conduct a presentation is how you wrote your book. If your book doesn't instil confidence, they'd rather go with a safe bet than take a chance on you.

By contrast, if you have a clear structure you sound more intelligent, thoughtful and organised. You sound like you actually have the qualifications and experience you list in your bio. A clear structure even improves your sense of humour, because any jokes or sly remarks naturally build on the surrounding content.[17]

But the greatest benefit of a clear structure is that it makes you sound like you know what you're talking about.

---

17   I'd insert a joke or sly remark here, but I'm not clever enough.

Structure guides your content

When most entrepreneurs set a word-count target and writing schedule, they encounter two issues.

The first is not having enough content – they breeze through their first 10,000 to 15,000 words only to hit a wall. They either touch on a lot of areas without going into depth, or they cover a handful of areas in depth yet completely forget others that would have been highly relevant.

The second issue is they have enough words, but they are the wrong ones. They include content that is interesting but isn't relevant to their ideal readers or related to the main subject of their book. Or they include the right content, but they repeat it in several different places. When it comes to editing, this is a recipe for aggressive cutting.

If they'd started with a clear structure, this wouldn't have happened.

A clear structure would not only have outlined every topic they needed to cover, but would have listed the key questions they needed to answer for each topic to ensure they discussed them in depth.[18] By seeing the outline of their book as a list of ideas, they could easily see if topics were included more than once (or if they were missing) and address this in the planning stage, rather than struggling to navigate an eighty-page document.

---

18   More on this in Chapter 5.

Structure smooths the writing process

In one writing montage, the writer stares at his computer screen. The cursor blinks at the beginning of an empty page. He twiddles a pen between his fingers. He spins on his chair. He gazes out the window. He leaves and comes back with a coffee. He scrunches up a sheet of paper and tosses it at the bin, only to miss. He tries again, sinks the goal and throws his arms in the air at his victory, commentating on his feat as his imaginary audience goes wild.

Meanwhile, the page stays blank.

In a second writing montage, uplifting music plays. The writer is busy tapping away, taking sips of coffee and eating lunch over her keyboard. When someone tries to call her away, she shakes them off – she's on a roll and wants to get the job done. The sun goes down and comes back up, and she's still typing.

In the next scene, she sits in her desk chair with a cardboard box on her lap. As she opens it, a choir of angels sings and a golden light shines from above. The camera pans, and inside the box we see copies of her freshly printed book.

A clear structure is the key to being the second writer, as – if you do it right – there's very little writing to do.

So how do you sort your structure before you start writing?

That's what this section is for. By now you have chosen a book idea that hits the sweet spot, and have matched it to one of the five book types. In this section I'll take you through how each of the five book types is structured, followed by how to organise your body chapters, introduction and conclusion, and what to include in each.

Are you ready to get started?

CHAPTER 4

Your big picture structure

Nonfiction books are typically structured with an introduction at the beginning, a conclusion at the end, and then some stuff in the middle.

In every case, your introduction and conclusion focus on the general subject of your book, while the 'stuff in the middle', or your chapters, cover smaller topics that come under the broad umbrella of your book's subject.

One of the mistakes a lot of new authors make is only considering the broad subject of their book, rather than the related topics they need to discuss to cover that subject in depth. This leads to a lot of waffling and repetition. After all, there's only so much you can write about a general subject. How many ways can you say that self-esteem is important to women? How many ways can you say that small businesses are great? How many ways can you say that growing avocado trees is a challenge?

It's only by breaking your broad subject down into smaller chapter topics – the most important topics you think your readers need to understand in order to grasp your broad subject – that you can create a discussion that will give your readers value.

What does this look like in practice? If your book's broad subject was financial planning, your chapter topics might include areas like:

- Paying off debt
- Lowering your expenses
- Saving
- Investing
- Automating your finances

If your book's subject was improving your health, your chapter topics might include:

- Diet
- Exercise
- Mindset
- Stress
- Sleep

If your book's subject was planning the perfect wedding, your chapter topics might include:

- Venues
- Catering
- Wardrobe
- Photography
- Music

If you did the mind-mapping exercises in Part 1, you should already have a clear idea of the topics that will help explain your broad idea in detail – they are the second-level ideas on your mind map. If you haven't done those exercises, please go back and do them now.

Done? Good. Let's move on.

These smaller topics, or chapters, will be the bulk of your content. And just as this content will vary depending on the type of book you write, so too will the organisation of this content.

If you chose a book type in Chapter 2, feel free to jump straight to the section on the structure of that book type. If not, work through each of the exercises in this chapter. As you start fleshing out the structure of your book, you will find that one book type will come more naturally to you than others. This is the book type you should focus on as you create your book blueprint.

1. The how-to book

The body of a how-to book focuses on practical advice for the reader so that they can achieve the result your book promises. The most effective way to deliver that advice is by grouping it into steps or areas.

There is an expression that a confused customer never buys. You could also say that a confused student never acts. When someone is Google-ing your area of expertise, they will be confronted by thousands, even millions, of search results. While they may make a valiant effort, it's difficult and time consuming to absorb even a small part of that information, let alone to figure out how to apply it to their unique situation. By grouping your advice into sequential steps or key areas, you do the work for them. You decide which information is the most relevant and will make the biggest difference to their situation, you organise it in the most effective way, and you tell them which actions they can take to get the best results.

Grouping your content into steps, also known as 'chunking', can improve your readers' learning process as well. A 1956 paper titled 'The Magical Number Seven, Plus or Minus Two: Some Limits on Our Capacity for Processing Information', written by cognitive psychologist George A Miller, found that people find it easier to remember smaller numbers of content items containing more information than larger numbers of content items, even if those items contained less information.[19] As far as your book is concerned, this means it's easier for your readers to remember five to nine large steps, which might each contain a lot of information, rather than trying to remember thirty separate pieces of advice. Recalling one of the larger steps then triggers the memory of the information contained within that step, making it easier for your readers to gain a more holistic understanding of your subject.

From your perspective, a clear process is also ownable. With the amount of free information available online, it's difficult to claim to be the only expert in your area. How many people are already claiming to be experts

---

19   George A Miller, 'The Magical Number Seven, Plus or Minus Two: Some Limits on our Capacity for Processing Information', *Psychological Review* 63 (1956), 81–97.

on leadership or business development or nutrition? However, you *can* become the only expert in your industry-recognised five-step framework. Being recognised as the creator of this system then makes the system, and your knowledge, more valuable. Readers don't have the time to sift through hundreds of thousands of search results, and they don't have the time to figure out how to apply all of this information to their own situation. By giving your readers a straightforward formula, you will be answering their prayers for something they can easily understand that *works*, and they will pay top dollar to access it.

So how do you do this? I've found two approaches work well for organising your content: the sequential process, and the topic hierarchy.

The sequential process is when you organise your content into steps the reader needs to follow to achieve their goal. Each step becomes a chapter or a part of the book.

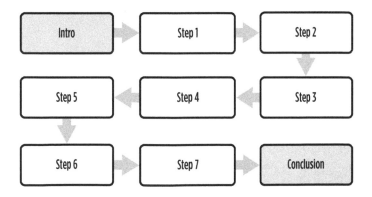

For example, in *Property Prosperity*, author Miriam Sandkuhler has seven chapters that cover the seven steps readers need to take to invest like an expert. In *Nail It!*, author Adam Hobill discusses the ins and outs of building a home in four parts: the Idea Stage, the Design Stage, the Quote Stage and the Build Stage. Each of these stages is then broken into smaller chapters.

However, you might find that you have a lot of practical advice but it doesn't fit cleanly into a sequential process. In this case, think about whether you can group your advice by topic, area or principle.

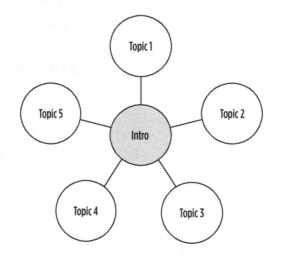

A great example of a topic-based structure is Stephen Covey's classic *The 7 Habits of Highly Effective People*, which covers seven ways of being for personal success, rather than a seven-step formula. In a similar vein, the book you're reading is split into four key areas: idea, structure, content and language.

As these topics may not be sequential, the best way to organise them is hierarchically. This might mean:

- Start with the most important topic, and work your way down to the least important topic.

- Start with the largest topic, and work your way down to the smallest topic.

- Start with the most basic topic, and work your way up to the most complex topic.

In any case, the content covered at the beginning of the book should pave the way for the content that comes later in the book. In this book, for example, it wouldn't have made sense to have started discussing your book's content or language before you had a clear book idea. Therefore, the idea, as the broadest or most basic topic, needed to be covered before the more detailed topics.

Action time – Your how-to mind map

Take out the how-to mind map you created in Chapter 2. You should have your book idea, written in a how-to phrase, in the centre of the page, with second-level ideas branching out from it.

Looking at these second-level ideas, or chapter topics, ask yourself: do you have a sequential process, or are your second-level ideas key areas or topics?

Once you have decided whether you have a sequential process or key topics, then think about the order in which they would best be covered. Which step or topic should come first? Which topics are dependent on other topics being understood?

Write a number next to each topic on your mind map, indicating the order in which you'll cover them.

2. The thought leadership book

In 1995, psychologists Roy Baumeister and Mark Leary published a paper that discussed humans' innate need to belong.[20] They discovered that we readily form relationships with others without any material incentives, once we form those relationships we are reluctant to break them (even in abusive situations), and that those who lack meaningful close relationships with others suffer – married couples were healthier, experienced less stress and were more likely to live longer, while being separated from loved ones caused distress, sadness and loneliness.

Our desire to belong is so strong that we seek it out – not only in relationships, but through the products we buy, the communities we join and the companies we work for. As Simon Sinek wrote in *Start with Why*, 'Our desire to feel like we belong is so powerful that we will go to great lengths, do irrational things and often spend money to get that feeling.'[21]

What does this have to do with your book?

We feel like we belong by connecting with people who we think are like us. They might wear the same clothes, have the same interests or share the same culture. Above all else, though, they believe what we believe.

Thought leadership books communicate what you believe and why you believe it, which gives your readers the ability to subscribe to those beliefs and to form

---

20   Roy F Baumeister & Mark R Leary, 'The need to belong: Desire for interpersonal attachments as a fundamental human motivation', *Psychological Bulletin* 117 (1995), 497-529.
21   Simon Sinek, *Start with Why*, (New York: Penguin, 2009), 53.

communities and movements around them. This makes them a powerful way to fulfil their need to belong to something greater than themselves.

So how do you do it?

Thought leadership books are often broken into parts, which cover:

- An education on your philosophy and the evidence that supports your beliefs,

- The problems your readers are experiencing and how your philosophy can solve them, and

- The benefits your readers will experience as a result of adopting your philosophy.

Action time – Your thought leadership mind map

Take out the thought leadership book mind map you created in Chapter 2. Get three different coloured pens and circle the following:

- Colour 1 – circle the educational content. What do you need to teach your readers before you can persuade them to subscribe to your philosophy?

- Colour 2 – circle the problem content. What have you written that is a problem your target readers may be experiencing?

- Colour 3 – circle the benefit content. What are the benefits of them solving these problems?

The first part, or the educational piece, outlines your philosophy and shares the reasons why you believe this. If your philosophy is very different to the beliefs that most people subscribe to, or is unfamiliar to your target readers, then you'll need to back up your reasoning with a lot of evidence to persuade them and build your credibility.

The second part delves deep into your ideal readers' problems. You may have one chapter per problem, and these chapters will also use a lot of evidence-based content to explain the problem in detail and its ramifications. For example, if you were writing a book on natural health and you felt one of the problems with our health is the modern-day sedentary lifestyle, you could describe how sedentary our lives have become (such as facts on the number of hours the average adult spends sitting each day), why this has happened (such as technological developments over the past few decades), and the likely consequences (such as weight gain).

The third part would then go into the benefits of solving these problems, with one chapter on each benefit, again using a lot of evidence-based content to make your case. Depending on the amount of content you have, the second and third part could be combined where each chapter covers both the problem and the benefits of solving that problem.

In each of these parts, I recommend following a hierarchical structure. This might mean:

- Start with the most important topic, and work your way down to the least important topic.

- Start with the largest topic, and work your way down to the smallest topic.

- Start with the most basic topic, and work your way up to the most complex topic.

In some cases, you might have a final part where you discuss your practical framework at a high level. Unlike in a how-to book, where you would have a chapter or part on each step of your framework, in a thought leadership book you'd have just a couple of paragraphs on each. If you are planning a series of two books – one thought leadership book and one how-to book – this can be a great way to start building your credibility and create an audience for your second book.

Action time – Your list book mind map

Take out the list book mind map you created in Chapter 2. Can your tips and tricks be grouped into larger topics or categories?

1. Grab some coloured pens.

2. Think about some broad topics into which you can group your tips.

3. Pick one colour and write down the name of that topic on the mind map. Circle any tips related to that topic in that colour.

4. Take a second colour and write down a second topic. Circle any tips related to that topic in that colour.

5. Continue this process until you have circled most, if not all, of your tips.

6. Consider how these areas would best be organised. Is there a clear hierarchical

> structure for your topics? If so, number each of the topics in the order in which you'll cover them in your book.
>
> Now that you have grouped your tips into broad topics, this is a great opportunity to see if those topics inspire any new tips. Any ideas? Write them down.

Now this is all a bit theoretical, so what does it look like in practice?

In Part 1 I mentioned Lissa Rankin's *Mind over Medicine* as an excellent example of a thought leadership book. Her book is structured in three parts. The first part covers the basic idea that our minds can heal our bodies and the evidence behind this theory (in other words, this is the part on education).

The second part discusses the various areas where this can be seen in our lives, such as in our relationships, careers and emotional states (this covers the areas where readers might be experiencing problems, and the benefits of solving those problems, which is all backed up by evidence from medical journals).

The third part briefly introduces her six-step process to healing ourselves.

3. The list book

While list books are designed to be opened and read at any page, they can't simply be a random selection of tips –

like any book type, they need structure and organisation to help your readers find what they need.

The easiest way to do this is by grouping your tips into topics, much like how-to books that cover areas or principles rather than sequential steps. Then, once your tips are grouped, start with the most general, least advanced piece of advice, and progressively get more advanced and more specific as you move through your tips.

Andrew Griffiths is one example of an author who has built his reputation on list books, having published twelve books that have sold in over sixty countries. His *101 tips* books include *101 Ways to Market Your Business*, *101 Ways to Advertise Your Business*, *101 Ways to Sell More of Anything to Anyone* and more. While all of these contain a lot of information and can be opened on any page, the reason they work is because the tips have been grouped into broader topics. If we look at *101 Ways to Advertise Your Business* as an example, the tips are grouped in the following topics:

- Advertising in newspapers
- Making television advertising work for you
- Have some fun on radio
- Telephone directories
- High-impact outdoor signage
- Direct mail advertising
- Advertising in magazines
- Advertising with other businesses
- Writing your advertisement
- Using the internet to advertise your business

Another example is Justine Waddington's *Solo Traveller's Compass*, which covers over 200 practical tips for first-time solo travellers. Like Andrew, Justine organises her tips into related themes with three main parts to the book (Getting Started, Before You Go, and On Your Trip), and chapters within those parts on topics such as: whether or not to share a room; passports, visas and insurance; and how to stay healthy and safe while you travel.

4. The interview book

Interview books are a great way to engage readers in a story that shares a range of perspectives. The way you organise these books depends on the story you want them to tell.

If you are sharing a sequential story then the interviews could be organised sequentially, either based on when the person was interviewed or the period they discuss in their interview. If it's a story that covers a number of themes or lessons, then the interviews could be organised according to those themes or lessons. If the interviews focus on a single area, then a hierarchical structure could work well, where you start with the most high-level interview and then choose interviews that go into more depth as you progress through the book.

The challenge is creating a cohesive story that links all of the interviews together, as this is what sets mediocre interview books apart from those that are a great read. Achieving this goes beyond simply organising the interviews. You may need to:

- Add introductory and concluding content to the start and end of each interview or theme,

- Add linking content between interviews, explaining how each one builds on the previous one, or highlighting the differences between them,

- Edit the interviews to cut superfluous content that doesn't contribute to your main message, and

- Rewrite the interviews so they capture the atmosphere of the interview and the character of the interviewee.

By adding these details, you can make interviews read like more of a story, so the reader can imagine you sitting down with the interviewee, rather than sticking to a dry question-and-answer format.

In Part 1 I mentioned Monique Bayer's *Devouring Melbourne* as an example of an interview book done well. In her book she shares the experience of each interview, describing what it was like to sit down with the owner of each restaurant and cafe she visited.

How does she structure her interviews? She starts with the topics of food, coffee and wine, then breaks food down further into the major food types featured in her tours: Italian, Chinese and chocolates. She introduces each type of food (or drink) by explaining how it made its way to Melbourne and the part it plays in Melbourne's food culture today, creating a cohesive story about the city's relationship with food.

Action time – Your interview book mind map

Take the interview mind map you created in Chapter 2 and review the interviewees you have listed. Can you group them by common themes? What story would you like to tell, and how can each interviewee contribute to that story?

Now, start organising:

1. Circle the names of any interviewees who could be grouped in the same colour.

2. Think about how you can link them to create a compelling narrative. What will you need to add in between interviews to build your story? Make some notes on this now.

---

5. The memoir

If you've decided to write a memoir, the first step to writing a great one is ensuring you have a clear, reader-friendly structure. Unless you have an extraordinary experience you'd like to unveil or explore, the most effective way to structure your memoir is around a key lesson or message you want to share.

Structuring your story around a key lesson or message has a number of benefits, for both you and your readers.

From your perspective, the lesson or message you choose will act as a filter. It will help you choose which stories to include and which to cut, and which could be developed in more detail with research and interviews.

This will save you a lot of time and heartache in the writing and editing process. When writing, you simply won't write stories that aren't necessary, which means you can focus on fleshing out the ones that are. When it comes to editing, your editor is less likely to cut content that doesn't fit and is less likely to find large holes you need to fill because you've already included the right content.

Having a clear lesson or message behind your memoir will also act as a marketing tool. Whenever someone asks what your book is about, rather than simply saying 'my story', it can be a book about overcoming post-natal depression or discovering how to adapt to the French way of life. This not only makes it easy for the person you're speaking with to figure out whether your book is something they're interested in, it also makes it easier for them to spread the word to others.

From your readers' perspective, a single lesson or message gives them a reason to read, as those who are already interested in and have already read books about that topic are likely to gravitate towards other books that share a similar message. This focus also creates more value, as your reader will feel they have learnt something by reading, rather than simply running through a chronological list of experiences.

Once you have your central lesson or message, how do you structure your stories?

Your introduction and conclusion should focus on that lesson or message, as this will help provide a container for everything that comes in the middle. As for those middle bits, either a sequential or a topic-based structure can work quite well.

A sequential structure would focus on sharing a period of your life that is relevant to your core message or lesson in a chronological order. One example of a sequential memoir done well is Llew Dowley's *Crazy Mummy Syndrome*. Nine weeks after the birth of her son, Llew's three-year-old daughter wouldn't stop crying. Llew hadn't showered, hadn't eaten and had barely slept. She begged her daughter to stop crying, just for a minute. Eventually she snapped and screamed, '*Shut up, shut up, shut up!*' Two days later she was diagnosed with postnatal depression. The story that follows is her pursuit of happiness, which culminates in raising $10,000 for the Black Dog Institute.

Meanwhile, a topic-based structure would break your core message or lesson into smaller topics, so that each chapter focuses on a particular topic and shares the experiences and stories related to that topic. An example of a topic-based memoir is *Almost French* by Sarah Turnbull. A twenty-seven-year-old journalist from Sydney, Sarah's story started when she arrived at Charles de Gaulle airport in Paris to meet a French man she'd met in Romania several months before. Overcome with anxiety, the chance encounter turns into a romance that leads to her starting a new life in Paris. Her book then describes her journey to become almost French, with each chapter reflecting on a different element of French life – social gatherings, fashion, the food, customer service and more – and countless cultural clashes along the way.

In both of these examples, notice that neither author wrote about her life in general – both were focused on telling a single story.

Action time – Your memoir mind map

Take the memoir mind map you created in Chapter 2 and think about the message or theme you'd like to share. Is everything on the mind map related to this message, or are there anecdotes you've written down just because you think they're good stories, or you feel like you need to cover your entire life?

This is the time to be ruthless – cross out *everything* that is not related to your main message. Then focus on writing down more stories that are.

Turning your mind map into a blueprint

If you started this chapter unsure about which book type was the right one for you, now you should have more clarity. You probably found that the structure of one book type sparked more ideas for your chapters – practical steps or topics for a how-to book, educational and persuasive content for a thought leadership book, tips and tricks for a list book, interview topics and an overarching story for an interview book, or personal stories that demonstrate a lesson or message for a memoir.

The mind map you created for that book type will be the foundation of your book blueprint – the central idea is the subject of your book, and the second-level ideas will form your chapter topics. In the next chapter you'll look at how to break down those chapter topics in more detail, including how a chapter should be structured and the key questions you need to address to fill it out.

CHAPTER 5

Chapter structure made simple

Now that you have a book idea, a book type and an overall structure, the next step is mapping out your body chapters, or the chapters that come between your introduction and conclusion.

If you are tempted to just start writing, try to hold off for a little longer. Remember, your goal is to write a high-quality book that will make you stand out as a leader in your field. The best way to do that is to do all of the grunt work now – then the book will write itself.

By contrast, imagine if you started writing your book now. You would open up a blank document and type one of your chapter topics at the top of page one. Then what?

If you're like most people, there would be a lot of pen clicking, spider solitaire and staring out the window.

Why? Because you don't have a *system*. Essentially, you are in the same position as you were when you just had a vague book idea – expecting willpower and inspiration to get you through your first draft. Unfortunately, inspiration is unreliable, and willpower tends to fade when you don't make progress. And while inspiration and willpower might get you through a few hundred words, or even a few thousand, what happens when your inspirational well dries up? What happens when a difficult client drains your energy, or the kids are playing up, or you accidentally double book yourself?

When you have a system, however, you always know what to write. You don't need to spend hours thinking, waiting for divine intervention, or reading other people's material, because you've already mapped out everything you're going to cover in every single chapter. This means that you don't need to rely on inspiration. You don't need willpower to push yourself to write. In fact, you don't even need to think that much, because you did all of the thinking *before* you started writing.

Instead, all you need to do is expand your bullet points and answer the questions you raised in the planning process.

This chapter contains the most powerful pages in this book. This chapter is the difference between just pumping out words in the hope that some of them will be good and writing on purpose in a way that builds your credibility and converts your readers into loyal disciples (and, hopefully, paying clients!).

In this chapter, you're going to learn how to create your book blueprint.

So how do you do this? When it comes to structuring your body chapters, you need to keep two concepts in mind:

1. Every chapter should read like a mini-book.
2. For every subtopic, there are three key questions you must answer.

Each chapter = a mini-book

As I mentioned last chapter, nonfiction books consist of an introduction, a conclusion, and chapters in the middle. The introduction and conclusion focus on the general subject of your book, while the chapters in the middle delve into more specific topics that help expand your readers' understanding of that general subject.

Each of your body chapters works in the same way. Each chapter covers a broad topic that you introduce using a general introduction, explain in more depth by breaking it down into related subtopics, and then tie up with a general conclusion or chapter summary.

Let's return to the financial planning example from last chapter to help break this down. If your book's broad subject was financial planning, the introduction and conclusion would be on financial planning in general, while the chapter topics might cover areas like:

- Paying off debt
- Lowering your expenses
- Saving

- Investing
- Automating your finances

The same formula then applies to your chapters. The chapter on paying off debt would start with a general introduction on paying off debt, followed by subtopics that elaborate on this general subject, like:

- Prioritising your current debts
- Paying off debt with the snowball strategy
- Strategies to avoid debt in future

Once you have covered your subtopics, you would then summarise everything in a brief conclusion or chapter summary.

As a writer, this makes it easier for you to create a more in-depth discussion in each of your chapters. Just as it would have been a struggle to write 30,000 to 50,000 words about financial planning in general, breaking down your broad idea into topics gives you direction for a more detailed discussion. The same goes for your chapter – rather than having to write 5,000 words about paying off debt, by breaking your chapter topic into smaller subtopics, you can create a more detailed discussion.

This not only takes the pressure off you – as rather than having to think about 5,000-word chunks of writing you only need to think about 1,000-word chunks for each of your subtopics – it also creates more direction for your readers. By breaking down each of your broad topics into subtopics, you give them a system for learning the lesson or absorbing the message you want to convey. It's much easier to implement a three-step method for paying off debt than it is to simply be told about paying off debt in a general sense, without any concrete advice on how to do it.

How many subtopics does each chapter need?

As a general guide, the chapters in a 30,000- to 50,000-word book range from 2,500 to 5,500 words.[22]

There are two reasons for this range.

The first reason is to avoid information overload, both in the form of too much information in a single chapter, and too many chapters with very little information. Too much information in a single chapter makes it easy for your readers to lose track of the key message or lesson of that chapter – instead, they get lost in case study after case study, or personal anecdote after personal anecdote, only to get to the end of the chapter and not remember what they learnt.

Conversely, too many chapters with very little information raises a number of issues. The first is that if you have thirty chapters of 500 to 1,500 words each (or one to three A4 pages), you can only cover the chapter topics at a very high level. This means there's very little space to include evidence to persuade your readers to agree with your view, or practical advice that your readers can implement. As a result, the risk is that the reader has a frustrating reading experience

---

22 To give you an idea of how long this is, Chapter 1 in this book is about 5,700 words, so slightly over the range. By contrast, Chapter 2 is just under 3,000 words.

because they don't get the benefits they were expecting to get when they picked up your book. The second issue is that, even if the chapters are short, having thirty separate topics feels like a lot for your readers to remember, unlike when you chunk the same content into broader categories.

The second reason for a chapter word-count range is that ensuring all of your chapters fall within that range creates a sense of balance through your book. If your 50,000-word book has one 18,000-word chapter and every other chapter is around 3,000 words long, this skews your entire book towards a single topic. This then raises the questions of whether that single topic should have been a book in its own right, whether it should have been broken up into smaller chapters, and whether the smaller topics deserve to stand on their own as chapters if you can't discuss them in the same amount of detail. By aiming for a similar word count for every chapter, you demonstrate that each area or step is just as important as the others and deserves its place in your book.

So, if you focus on a 2,500- to 5,500-word range for each of your chapters, how many subtopics would that include? I find that between three and five subtopics works well. However, keep in mind that this is just a guideline – if you have two rather lengthy subtopics, or seven smaller tips you want to cover, this can also work well. The key is covering each subtopic in the right level of depth (more on this under *Three key questions*).

How to think of your subtopics

If you revisit the mind map you created for your chosen book type, you should have your book idea written in the centre of the page with second-level ideas branching out from it. These second-level ideas will be your chapter topics.

Now, depending on how inspired you were when you did that exercise, you may already have some third-level ideas branching off from your chapter topics. If so, great – you've got a head start on this exercise. If not, don't worry – you'll tackle it here.

When thinking about subtopics for your chapters, your focus should always be, 'what does my reader need to know to grasp this concept?' This might include:

- Steps – Is there a three-to-five-step process your readers can take to tackle this topic?

- Skills – Are there certain skills your reader needs to adopt in this area?

- Tips – Do you have a number of tips for either grasping or getting a head start on this topic?

- Criteria – Are there criteria your readers need to meet to fully understand or demonstrate their knowledge of this topic?

- Questions – Are there certain questions your readers need to think about relating to this topic?

- Ideas – Are there key ideas or concepts that help break down this topic?

None of these angles is better or worse than any other – they are just different ways of looking at your chapter topics. If you still find yourself struggling to think of subtopics after considering your chapters from all of these angles, take a look at some other books that address your subject and your audience for inspiration.

You can then organise these subtopics just as you organised the chapters in your book – sequentially, if appropriate, or in a hierarchical structure where you move from the most important subtopic to the least important one, or the broadest subtopic to the most detailed one.

Action time – Expand your mind map

Revisit the mind map for your chosen book type. You should have your book idea written in the centre of the page, with chapter topics branching out from that central idea.

1. For each chapter, think about three to five subtopics you need to discuss to fully cover the chapter topic. Write these on your mind map, branching out from the chapter topic.

2. How will you organise these subtopics? Sequentially or hierarchically? Number each of the subtopics within each chapter.

Hold onto this mind map for the next exercise, as you will use this as the starting point for your book blueprint.

Three key questions

Once you have a list of subtopics within each chapter, the next step is knowing what to write about each of them. When it comes to how-to books, list books and, to a certain extent, thought leadership books, I've found the easiest approach to this is answering the key questions – 'what', 'why' and 'how'.

What

'What' is simply explaining the topic you're discussing, and it can range from a single sentence to a couple of pages, depending on how complex your topic is and how familiar your target readers are with it.

Now if you're familiar with Simon Sinek and his theory on starting with 'why', this might seem to be a little backward. After all, in a world where most leaders and businesses focus on 'what', isn't it important to share 'why' to inspire action and loyalty?

In some situations, I agree with Sinek – a strong 'why' is a far more compelling way to begin than a barrage of technical specifications. When it comes to your chapter structure, though, I find it works best to start with 'what'.

When Sinek recommends starting with 'why', he often gives the example of a business pitch or an introduction. In this case, your 'why' can be a powerful way to begin. However, one of the reasons this works is because your pitch or introduction is likely to only run for a couple of minutes. This means you still get to your 'what' fairly quickly, giving your listeners the essential context they need to understand your 'why'.

When writing a chapter, you don't have the same restrictions as a sales pitch. If you start with 'why', you could potentially go on for several pages about why what you're writing about is so important, without your readers knowing what you're writing about! This leads to frustrated and confused readers who aren't likely to get the results they want from reading.

Your 'what' gives your readers this clarity. It gives them context and tells them what to expect, and this prepares them to read what comes next, which is your 'why'.

Why

In the context of your chapter, your 'why' is the reason the topic is important. In a thought leadership book, this will be the bulk of your content.

Most entrepreneurs don't include 'why' content, but they should. On one hand, I get it – you're already familiar with this content. You already know about why it's important. So it's easy to assume that your readers do too.

You can't make this assumption. Unless you're writing to existing clients, you need to assume that some people are brand new to your concepts and may need some persuading. In fact, even those who are familiar with your content could use another dose of 'why'; after all, the reason they're reading your book is because they haven't been getting results, so hammering home why they need to take action is essential to ensure they actually follow through.

What do I mean by 'why' content?

'Why' content is anything that makes your case for the importance of what you're writing about. This is often the benefits your readers will experience if they follow your advice and the potential consequences if they don't. It also includes evidence like case studies, examples and statistics, as these are proof of the benefits and consequences you list, or why what you're teaching is so important. (I'll discuss this in more detail in Part 3.)

How much 'why' content do you need? This depends on your book and how much you think your readers will object to your ideas and advice. If you're a naturopath writing a book about natural health, and you know that your readers already understand the importance of eating well but have a strong objection to exercise[23], a chapter on diet wouldn't need much 'why' content. A chapter on exercise, on the other hand, would require far more to persuade your readers.

Katherine Maslen did this well in *Get Well, Stay Well* when she described sitting as the new smoking. According to one of the studies she referenced, every hour of seated TV-watching cuts twenty-two minutes from your life, while each cigarette reduces a smoker's life span by eleven minutes.[24] As someone who's quite good with her diet but quite lazy with exercise, this 'why' content was powerful enough to make me get up and go for a jog!

---

23   I can hear it now … 'Do I *have* to?'
24   Katherine Maslen, *Get Well, Stay Well* (South Australia: Griffin Press, 2014), 193.

How

In a how-to or list book, after 'why' comes 'how'.

The goal of someone buying these practical books is to learn how to achieve a certain result. Therefore, your 'how' content, or actionable advice, is extremely important because it gives your readers the tools they need to achieve that result. 'How' content is where they get the most value.

Until you give your readers this practical information, everything you've discussed is theoretical. And if you leave it out of a chapter, they might think, 'Well, that was nice, but now what?'

'How' content is anything that enables your readers to implement what you're teaching, including questions, activities and action items. (Again, I discuss this in more detail in Part 3.)

One great example of a practical book is Peita Diamantidis's *Finance Action Hero*. Peita shares detailed exercises in every chapter, which include activities like clearing away clutter and setting up a 'waterfall of cash' to pay off credit card debt. She also includes prompts in feature boxes for readers to write in their diary, links to the online tools she created to help with her readers' money management, and action items at the end of each chapter.

Why this works

This structure works because it is both clear and compelling. It's clear because your readers always know exactly what you're talking about and can easily follow your logic. It's compelling because, even though you start with 'what', your 'why' still comes early enough for them to be sold on your message. This means they are more likely to implement the steps you outline when you get into the 'how'.

Then if they actually implement what you teach, *that* means they are far more likely to say that what you teach works, and to turn into loyal clients and fans.

Putting it all together

If the two concepts for mapping out a well-structured chapter are that each chapter should read like a mini-book and the three key questions, how do you put them together? It's a matter of asking the right questions at the right time.

As I mentioned earlier, each chapter works like a mini-book, with an introduction, a conclusion and subtopics in the middle. The introduction of your chapter explains the general chapter topic (the 'what') including the reasons it is important (the 'why'), and then outlines what will be covered in the body of the chapter (your subtopics, or the 'how'). In each of your subtopics, you then discuss 'what' that subtopic is about, 'why' that subtopic is important, and 'how' your readers can take action on that subtopic. Finally, your chapter conclusion gives a quick recap on what your readers have learnt and the benefits of this before moving on to your next chapter.

In Christina Morgan-Meldrum's *Working Your Mojo*, for example, which teaches entrepreneurial skills to musicians, her first chapter was about goal setting. The chapter introduction explained the importance of goal setting. The subtopics then covered getting her readers clear on where they were, figuring out where they wanted to go, making their goals more specific with the SMART goal framework, and then breaking their larger goals into smaller milestones. Because each of these was a distinct topic, she delved into each one by ensuring each had their own explanation ('what'), benefits ('why') and exercises ('how').

Action time – Create your blueprint

This is when you will turn your mind map into a blueprint. You can do this on your computer or using a pen and paper. I recommend using a computer as this makes it easier to add new notes and content to your blueprint over the coming chapters. However, you can start with a pen and paper if this feels more natural to you.

1. Create a new document with a blank page for each chapter.

2. On the first page, type the chapter topic at the top of the page.

3. Type 'chapter introduction' as a second heading.

4. Under 'chapter introduction', briefly explain what the chapter is about.

5. After explaining what the chapter is about, list the reasons why this topic is important

to your readers. What are the benefits they might experience from learning about this topic, and what are the risks of neglecting it? Just write bullet points for the moment, leaving space under each point so you can elaborate on it later.

6. Next, outline what you will cover in this chapter – this can be as simple as listing your subtopics in one sentence.

7. Type 'chapter body' as the next heading.

8. Under 'chapter body', make headings for each of your subtopics, leaving space under each.

9. Under the first subtopic, explain what that topic is about.

10. Under the first subtopic, list why that subtopic is important for your readers. Keep in mind that these reasons should be specific to this subtopic – they shouldn't repeat the general reasons you covered at the beginning of the chapter.

11. For list and how-to books, note practical, actionable ideas for your readers. These might be exercises, action steps, thinking questions, activities, or even more subtopics to consider.

12. Repeat these steps for each subtopic.

13. To conclude the chapter, type a 'chapter conclusion' heading.

14. Under 'chapter conclusion', list the key points or topics covered in that chapter.

15. Repeat these steps for each chapter.

The birth of your blueprint

You now have an outline for the body of your book, or the beginnings of a book blueprint! Don't worry if things still feel a bit light at this stage – you will elaborate on this outline in Part 3, where I'll cover the different types of content you can add to the 'what', 'why' and 'how' sections of each of your chapter topics and subtopics.

For now, though, let's take a look at your introduction and conclusion.

Bonus resource

For a free chapter template to get you started on your blueprint, head to grammarfactory. com/bb-bonus

---

CHAPTER 6

Topping and tailing – intros and conclusions

Introductions and conclusions are often the most challenging parts of your book to write. While you've organised your body chapters and know how to cover them in depth, these chapters can't just appear out of nowhere. They need to be introduced to help your reader make the transition from their knowledge into yours, and they need to be concluded to create a sense of closure and accomplishment.

A mistake many entrepreneurs make when planning a book is only focusing on the body of their book – the key points they'll use to express their argument, which case studies would work well, which experts to quote, and so on – and they forget about their introductions and conclusions. In fact, when I recommended moving one author's content from her opening chapters to the beginning of her book, she said, 'Isn't the introduction just fluff?'

No, your introduction is not fluff. Your introduction is where you convince your readers to read the rest of your book. In fact, if you offer a couple of free chapters on your website or allow Amazon users to download a sample, your introduction is where you convince your readers to *buy* your book. And when it comes to enticing potential partners to collaborate with you, or media personalities to contact you for an interview, all they are likely to read is your introduction (if they open your book at all).

Meanwhile, without a conclusion your book can feel unfinished. If your book concludes with the final step in your framework, it can leave your readers feeling unfulfilled and unsure of what to do next. By contrast, an effective conclusion will remind your readers of what they have learnt, which creates a sense of achievement. It will outline the benefits they will experience if they continue to implement your advice, which reminds them of the value your book provided. And it will give advice on any next steps, which gives them confidence that they can continue their journey independently.

Why *wouldn't* you want to leave your readers feeling like that?

An intro to intros

No matter how valuable your subsequent content, your introduction is the piece that will turn readers into clients, fans, partners and opportunities. It's where you share:

- What your book is about,

- Why it is so important for your readers, and

- Why you're the best person to discuss your topic.

In short, your introduction is arguably the most important part of your book. So, how do you write a great introduction?

Like your chapters, there's a formula – just five steps to write something that's clear, compelling and coherent.

1. Poke your readers' pain points

In Chapter 1, I discussed the importance of understanding your readers' most burning problems so you could position your book as the solution to them. This is where you will use that information.

By starting with your readers' thorniest problems you immediately demonstrate that your book is relevant to them, and this persuades them to keep reading. The more accurately you can identify and describe these problems, the more you build your credibility as the expert who can solve them.

So how do you do this? There are a number of ways to tackle this, with each method building on the previous one.

The first method is fairly straightforward – simply outline the problems your reader is experiencing, either in a bullet-point list or over a couple of paragraphs. If you're a personal trainer or a nutritionist who is writing a book on how new mums can lose ten kilos, for example, the problems these mothers might be experiencing include poor fitness levels, fatigue and low confidence.

While this gets straight to the point and ensures you've ticked the 'problem' box, it doesn't make for a very compelling read. For that, you need to move on to method number two.

The second method is to describe the problems your reader is experiencing, but rather than just listing the facts, you bring them to life with emotive language. To continue the previous example, rather than simply writing that new mums can lack confidence when carrying extra baby weight, you might say they feel saggy, fat and unattractive (these were the actual words listed in a poll of 3,000 new mothers run by fashion website *A Beautiful Mummy* in 2011).[25]

How do you find the right words? If you've been in the same position as your readers, you might already have a good idea of how this feels. If not, speak to some people who are your target readers about what they're struggling with, and take note of the words and phrases they use to describe their problems.

The third method is to describe these problems in the context of the day-to-day events that happen as a result. Let's return to our new mum. What are the day-to-day issues she experiences because she hasn't lost the weight? If one of her problems is lacking confidence, an experience that demonstrates this problem might be going shopping for new clothes and not finding anything that fits. You can then make this more impactful by incorporating the words

---

25   Fiona Macrae, 'Baby blues: It takes 18 months for a new mother to "feel like a woman" again', *The Daily Mail*, January 13, 2011, accessed April 22, 2015, http://www.dailymail.co.uk/femail/article-1346105/New-mothers-18-months-feel-attractive-having-baby.html

you listed in the previous method to describe how she feels when she has this experience.

By taking these three steps, you already have the power to engage your readers from the get go. But if you'd like to really set yourself apart, the final method is sharing the experience of your target readers in a story.

'Can I help you?'

You jump as a perky sales assistant tries to get your attention.

'No thanks, I'm just browsing.' You plaster on a smile before turning back to the rack of tops. What size are you now? It's the first time you've been shopping since you gave birth, and you have no idea. Maybe you should just give up…

'Are you sure?'

The sales assistant is still there.

You grab the next top from the rack: 'I'll try this one.'

You rush to the change room, dragging the curtain shut behind you. You rip off your top and quickly pull the new one down over your arms… until it gets stuck. You wriggle, tug and contort your shoulders, but it won't budge.

You decide to surrender and change back into your original outfit, only to discover that you can't get the top off.

'Oh please no,' you mutter as you try to yank the straightjacket up your arms. Your face burns and you start to wish you'd never gone on this shopping expedition. You tug harder and hear a riiiiip!

'Is everything alright?' the sales assistant calls.

After that introductory story, you could then continue the discussion with the other problems your readers might be experiencing. By including a story like this, you build an emotional connection with your readers. You show that you can relate to what they are going through. And they think that you *get* them.

Can you see how much more powerful that is than simply writing a list of problems?

Action time – Poke your readers' pain points

Take out your book blueprint and add a page at the beginning for your introduction. Then revisit your notes from the reader test in Part 1. What are your target readers' thorniest problems? Describe them using each of the following four methods:

- List them,
- Describe them with emotive language,
- Give examples of how these problems might look in their day-to-day lives, and
- Bring them to life with a story.

---

2. Share the possibilities

So what do you do if your book doesn't solve a problem, but instead helps your readers achieve a desire? Simply follow the same four steps, but instead of bringing your readers' problems to life, bring their desires to life.

Let's use home automation as an example. The first step is to list some of the features your readers might enjoy after implementing their home automation solutions, such as better security, improved energy efficiency and cool lifestyle gadgets.

The second step is to make it emotive. What words might your readers use to describe how these features make them feel? Security might help them sleep at night. Being energy efficient might make them feel proud that they're doing their bit for the planet. The lifestyle gadgets might help them have fun or even show off to their mates.

The third step is translating these features and feelings into day-to-day experiences. They might be able to monitor their house from their smartphone at work. They might not need to worry about turning off the sprinkler system on a rainy day, because their garden system monitors the water in the soil and knows whether or not their plants need extra watering. Or, with the touch of a button, their home might automatically switch to 'entertain' mode with low lighting and soft music playing.

Again, these three steps are more than enough to whet your readers' appetites. However, if you want to go above and beyond, once again you can set the scene with a story.

The following extract is from Sam Buckby's book, *Homes with a Heartbeat*.

Picture yourself walking up to the front door of your home. You've just driven home, parked in the driveway, stepped out of your car and locked it behind you. It's the end of a wintry day and, as the sky darkens, the weather has plummeted to near freezing and you're looking forward to getting indoors.

For most people, the next step would be to open the door and enter a building that is dim, cool and somewhat unwelcoming. Not for you...

You pull the keys out of your pocket and press the UNLOCK button on the little key chain security pendant, similar to your electronic car key. A faint click of the door lock, the lights on the veranda come to life and through the windows you can see the entry, hall and kitchen lights slowly ramping up to your desired level.

Before you step inside you know it's going to be nice and warm. It's a Friday and you would normally get home sometime between 6:00 and 6:30pm. Thankfully, your home knows this and the heating came on thirty minutes before you pulled into your driveway.

You're not worried about your safety either. There have been no alerts on your smart phone to indicate that anyone has entered the house.

Being the over-analyser that you are, you decide to double-check anyway, pulling out your smart phone to view the log of each of the movement sensors as you progress up the path. As expected, nothing all day.

You push the front door open and you can hear that song you love so much coming down the hall. For a second you wonder who turned that on… Oh, that's right; your 'Most played' tracks always greet you in the evenings. At this point, you're probably thinking about how great your taste in music is!

You stroll to the kitchen where you start getting dinner prepared. You press 'Evening' on your interactive touch screen and the entry lights dim as the kitchen lights and the lamp beside the sofa come on in response. The blinds throughout the living area roll down and the volume of the music increases ever so slightly so you can bop around as you cook. Your partner is due home in twenty minutes or so, but you really don't mind if they are running a little late. You feel safe, comfortable and inspired.

You love coming home.[26]

If you started your introduction with your readers' problems, this step is still important, as you need to describe what their life might look like if they solved these problems.

---

26   Sam Buckby, *Homes with a Heartbeat* (Melbourne: Michael Hanrahan Publishing, 2015), 1–3.

Sharing the benefits of solving their problems immediately after you've fleshed out those problems helps emphasise how good your solution is, as your readers can clearly see the contrast against how bad their situation is.

How do you do it? Simply follow the first three steps – list the benefits, describe them with emotive language, and translate them into the day-to-day experiences your reader will have as a result of solving their problems. (Another story isn't necessary at this stage – if you include two in a row it can start to feel long winded.)

So if we return to our new mum who is struggling to lose the baby weight, what are the benefits of losing the weight? These might include having more energy, improved sleep, clearer skin, more regular eating habits, improved fitness and more confidence.

Then imagine how these benefits would feel in this mum's day-to-day life.

> *Imagine if you bounced out of bed every morning after a night of refreshing sleep, excited about the day ahead. Imagine if making food choices was easy – if your fridge was full of colourful food; your meals tasted delicious and left you satisfied; and you knew they were improving your health, strength and vitality every single day. Imagine loving the way you looked in the mirror and planning a shopping trip to buy new clothes at your pre-baby size.*

And, as an author, imagine how much more this reader is going to want to find out what comes next.

Action time – Share the possibilities

If your book promises to help your readers achieve a desire, describe what the end result would look like using the following four methods:

- List them,

- Describe them with emotive language,

- Give examples of how these desires might look in their day-to-day lives, and

- Bring them to life with a story.

If you have already poked your readers' pain points, share the benefits of solving the problems you described earlier, either listing them using emotive language or giving examples of how these benefits might manifest in your readers' day-to-day lives.

3. Position your book as the solution

The next step is to position your book as the Holy Grail that will solve their problem, help them achieve their desires, or both.

The good thing is that because you started with your readers' problems and desires, you've already done your sales pitch. You've already convinced your reader that they need a solution. All that's left to do is outline what you will cover in your book.

First, you will need a linking sentence to transition from your benefit content to the outline of your book. This could be as simple as 'So where should you start?', or 'I've found there are X simple steps to achieve these benefits'.

Then you can outline your book. Simply write a subheading for each chapter or part of your book. If you are planning to have smaller chapters grouped within larger parts, I recommend just outlining the major parts here, as the list can start to get very long otherwise.

Then under each subheading write two to three sentences that explain what your readers will learn in each of these chapters or parts and the benefits they will experience as a result.

Action time – Outline your book

Using your blueprint as a guide, list the different chapters or parts of your book. Under each item on this list, make a note of:

- The main lessons your reader will learn
- The benefits of learning these lessons

---

4. Establish your credibility

Now you've shown your readers that you understand their problems, have started to build their hopes about what their lives might be like if they solved these problems, and have positioned your book as the solution that will help them achieve this. The logical next question for any sceptic is, 'Who are you to make all of these claims?'

This is where you share your credibility. This might include:

- Your education – do you have a degree or other qualifications in your area of expertise?

- Your experience – how many years have you been working in this field (both in your business as well as prior experience)? How many clients have you worked with? What type of clients are they – individuals like your readers, or global businesses?

- Your results – what results have your clients seen after implementing the recommendations you will be making in your book?

- Your story – how has your story informed your knowledge? Did you go through a personal journey like the one your reader is experiencing? What did you discover, and what results have you experienced?

In most cases, your education and experience is plenty to cement your credibility, and results your clients have experienced are a bonus that gives you the opportunity to hammer home the benefits your readers will likely experience after reading your book.

Just think about how you felt when I mentioned that I'd worked with over 100 entrepreneurs, that I'd been working as a professional writer and editor for eight years, and that I was going to teach you the same method I used to write this book. It probably put your mind at ease and reassured you that the advice to come was not only reliable, but that it had been tested and was therefore likely to work for you.[27]

I recommend having a good think about how relevant your story is in your introduction. In personal development books, personal stories can work quite well, as your personal journey is often the foundation of what you teach. Explaining how you started in the same position as your target readers, your trial and error to find a solution, and what you experienced when you discovered what actually *worked* can be an inspiration for readers who feel like they've tried everything and nothing has worked. It can also give them hope – if they see that you were just like them, it makes your solution feel more attainable.

However, if the advice you are sharing in your book *isn't* based on a personal journey then a lot of your story won't be relevant. If you are giving marketing advice, for example, your readers don't really need to know about your struggle to find a fulfilling career and why marketing was the right choice for you. That story doesn't contribute to your credibility as a marketing expert.

Instead, it's far more relevant to stick with your education, experience and results, as these are what demonstrate that your advice works.

---

27   At least, I hope that's how you felt. If you didn't, please don't say anything – I'm not sure my ego can take it.

Action time – Establish your credibility

Write down the main points you need to cover to demonstrate your credibility, including:

- Your education

- Your experience

- Your results

If you are writing a personal development book, or a book where your personal journey has informed your solution, you can also include your personal story.

However, remember to focus on the story that is relevant to your readers, which should be directly related to the content in your book.

5. Final note

While this isn't essential, you don't want your introduction to end abruptly, so it's nice to add a final note before going into the rest of the book.

This can be as simple as wishing your readers well and hoping they enjoy the book, or a couple of sentences recapping the benefits they'll experience before inviting them to get started.

What about the conclusion?

Like the introduction, the conclusion is another element that is often forgotten.

The purpose of your conclusion is to create closure for your readers – without it, they can feel like your book ended suddenly with no guidance on what to do next. By recapping what your readers have learnt and sharing next steps, your readers will feel more prepared to take those steps.

So what do you include in the conclusion? This can vary depending on what you've included in the body of your book. However, some common elements include a client case study, a summary of your book, the benefits your readers can expect, and any next steps they should take.

1. A client case study

Throughout the body of your book you'll use both personal and client examples to prove that your method works (more on this in Part 3). However, because you'll want each example to relate specifically to the current chapter, each example will probably only touch on a single step of the journey.

If you have a client who has taken every step of your process and has experienced outstanding results, this is a good chance to share their journey, including where they started, what they did, and the benefits they experienced from following your process.

Action time – Share a client case study

Go to the last page of your blueprint to outline your conclusion.

If you have a client who has taken every step of your process, or addressed every area in your book, who has experienced outstanding results, consider kicking off your conclusion with their story.

To get started, write down:

- Their original situation and the problems they were experiencing
- The steps they took or areas they addressed to change this situation (these steps or areas should align with the chapters in your book)
- The results they experienced after taking these steps

If your book covers a new model and you don't have a client who has completed every single one of your steps yet, don't stress – a case study is optional. As long as you cover the subsequent elements, you will still conclude on a positive note.

2. A summary

The key part of a conclusion is a summary of what your readers have learnt by reading your book. Just as you described each section or chapter in a paragraph in the introduction, you can do the same here.

Keep in mind that you need to vary the tone of this, rather than simply copying and pasting your introductory text. In the introduction, your goal was to build anticipation about everything your readers would learn. Here, your goal is for your readers to feel a sense of accomplishment and confidence – even if they haven't taken all of your action steps yet, now they know what to do to change their situation. This then leads into the benefits they'll experience as a result...

Action time – Summarise your book

Once again, outline the chapters or areas in your book. Ensure that you focus on the fact that your readers have already learnt this – rather than building anticipation, you want to create a sense of accomplishment.

3. The benefits your readers can expect

What are the benefits your readers should expect once they implement your advice? Giving a quick recap of the benefits will not only help your book finish on a high, but it will also give your readers that bit of extra motivation they may need to actually start taking your advice, rather than simply putting your book down once they finish.

Action time – Reinforce the benefits

Outline the benefits your readers will experience. Keeping in mind that this is just a recap, you won't need to go into as much detail as you did in the introduction. Instead, just focus on listing the benefits and incorporating some emotive language to reignite your readers' motivation.

---

4. Next steps

What should your readers do *after* reading your book? What comes after your five to nine steps?

Quite often there will be steps that don't quite fit in the body of your book, but which you think are important for your readers to recognise. These might include ongoing activities like maintenance and measuring progress, or they could include advice about the processes that come after your process.

A great example of this is the conclusion of Christina Morgan-Meldrum's *Working Your Mojo*, which I mentioned earlier. *Working Your Mojo* teaches entrepreneurial skills to musicians, and the book finishes on a great note by discussing how her readers will know when it is time to leave their day jobs and start working on their music full time.

> **Action time – Share the next steps**
>
> List any next steps your readers should think
> about after finishing your book, including:
>
> - Ongoing maintenance steps – how
>   can they maintain their progress?
> - Processes that come after the
>   framework outlined in your book –
>   who should they work with or what
>   should they do after completing all of
>   the steps?

Book ends for your book

You've now created a container for your book – an
introduction to familiarise your readers with your idea
and persuade them to keep reading, and a conclusion to
give them a sense of closure and accomplishment.

When done well, you'll see that the introduction and
conclusion are the finishing touches that transform your
book from being an unconnected collection of blog posts
or essays to being a cohesive piece of work that comes
together to deliver a clear message. So, if you haven't
already, go back to your blueprint and add a page at the
beginning to map out your introduction, and a page at the
end for your conclusion. Don't skip this – it's important.

Once you've done that, you can move on to elaborating
on your blueprint with content.

1. Your book should have an introduction, a conclusion, and some 'stuff in the middle'. The organisation of those middle chapters depends on the book type you choose.

   - How-to books:
     - o Revisit your how-to mind map. Do your second-level ideas, or chapter topics, form a sequential process, or are they key areas or topics?
     - o Which of these steps/topics should come first? Which are dependent on other topics being understood?
     - o Number each step/topic in the order in which you'll discuss them.
   - Thought leadership books:
     - o Revisit your thought leadership mind map.
     - o Circle educational content in one colour. What else do you need to teach your readers before you can persuade them to subscribe to your philosophy?
     - o In a second colour, circle the problem content. What other related problems might your target reader be experiencing?
     - o In a third colour, circle the benefit content. What are the benefits of them solving these problems?

- List books:
  - o   Revisit your list book mind map. Can your tips and tricks be grouped into larger topics?
  - o   Using coloured pens, write down some broad topics relating to your tips on your mind map. For every topic, circle any tips relating to that topic in that colour.
  - o   How could these areas be organised? Is there a clear hierarchical structure for your topics? If so, number each of the topics in the order in which you'll cover them in your book.
- Interview books:
  - o   Review the interviewees you have listed on your interview mind map. Can you group them by common themes? What story would you like to tell, and how can each interviewee contribute to that story?
- Memoirs:
  - o   Review your memoir mind map, considering the main message or theme you'd like to share. Is everything on the mind map related to this message, or are there anecdotes you've written down just because you think they're good stories, or you feel like you need to cover your entire life?

- Cross out everything that is not related to your main message.

- Write down more stories that are related.

2. Organise your chapters like mini-books:

   - For thought leadership, list and how-to books, create a blueprint document on your computer with one page for each chapter topic.

   - On each page, create the subtitles 'chapter introduction', 'chapter body' and 'chapter conclusion'.

   - Under the 'chapter body' subtitles, list three to five subtopics you need to discuss to fully cover the chapter topic, organising them sequentially or hierarchically.

3. For each of your chapter topics and subtopics, ask:

   - What – what are you writing about, in one sentence?

   - Why – why is this topic important? What are the benefits if your readers implement this advice? What are the risks if they don't?

   - How – what practical advice can you give them?

   - Type your notes for each of these questions in your blueprint.

4. Map out your introduction:

- Poke your readers' pain points – what are they struggling with that your book will solve?

- Share the possibilities – if your book helps your readers achieve a goal, rather than helping them solve a problem, bring that goal to life here. If your book helps solve a problem, explain the benefits of solving that problem here.

- Position your book as the solution – outline your book, using the chapters you've already mapped out as a guide.

- Give your credibility – share why you are the best person to be writing this book, including your education, experience, results and story.

- Final note – wish your readers well to lead into the body of your book.

5. Map out your conclusion:

- Write notes for a relevant client case study, if you have one.

- Summarise your book.

- List the benefits your readers can expect now that they have this knowledge.

- List any next steps.

PART 3

THE RIGHT CONTENT

CHAPTER 7

Fleshing out the skeleton

A few years ago I sat in an audience of 550 people watching Australia's leading small business author, Andrew Griffiths, deliver a one-hour presentation about the benefits of getting published. He talked about increasing your credibility, forming strategic partnerships, charging higher rates and getting more clients ... but I was unconvinced. I'd been immersed in the online marketing world for years at that time, and – while I was developing content – my content focused on blog posts, webinars, videos and e-courses.

Then someone raised a hand and asked the question at the front of my mind: 'Couldn't you just write an eBook?'

Andrew paused, walked over to the lectern, and picked up a book from the top of his stack of publications.

The room was silent as he returned to the centre of the stage, lifted the book over his head... and dropped it.

Thud! It landed at his feet.

'That's called "thud value",' hc said, 'and you can't do that with an eBook.'

The reason hard-copy books are so much more powerful than eBooks is they are tangible. You can physically hand a book to someone. This act of physically giving someone a book triggers a subconscious desire to reciprocate. If you buy me a drink, the next is my shout. If we have you around for a barbeque, the next time will be at your place. If you hand me your business card, I give mine back.

The greater the gesture, the more of an impact it has.

Think about it – if someone hands you a business card, you'll generally take a quick look at the design and details as your fingertips register the quality of the paper. If someone gives you a brochure or booklet instead, suddenly they stand out from everyone else at the event who just has a card. They seem more established and credible. It's almost like the weight of their reputation is in direct proportion to the weight of the booklet.

If they hand over a book instead, they move into another league entirely. As you now know, publishing a book is one of the quickest ways to become an industry authority. The ability to write a book clearly shows your expertise, and producing a high-quality book demonstrates the quality of the work you do in your business. And because most people haven't written one, becoming a published author means you automatically stand out.

If you've completed both the idea worksheet and the structure worksheet you should now have an outline of your chapters, the subtopics within each chapter, and bullet points to answer the three key questions for each subtopic. This organised collection of ideas is the skeleton of your book.

While you could start writing now, writing at this stage in your book blueprint often leads to a pattern of stop-and-start writing. You start your writing for the day, realise you need an example, and turn to Google or start looking through past client work to find one. Suddenly the hour you set aside for writing is up – it's time to get back to business, and you've only written a paragraph.

Or you will finish expanding your bullet points into sentences but only have a 10,000 to 15,000 word manuscript – in other words, a short booklet or eBook. And while a booklet is a step above a business card, it wouldn't make the same thud if you dropped it on the floor in a quiet room. To truly make an impact, to truly make a *thud*, you need to add some content.

What do I mean by content? Content is the flesh that will bulk up the skeleton of your book, and involves adding 'what' content (explanation), 'why' content (evidence) and 'how' content (exercises) to the list of bullet points you have created.

Explanation

As I discussed in Part 2, 'what' content explains the topic you're discussing and is important because it helps create context for your reader. This becomes the foundation for you to persuade them with your 'why' content so they will implement your 'how' content.

In many cases, you won't need a great deal of 'what' content. If your readers have been experiencing the same problems or trying to reach the same desires for some time, there's a good chance they already have some knowledge around your area of expertise. This will make explaining many of your topics redundant. (For example, terms like 'leadership' and 'goals' usually don't need explanation.) In these cases, referring to your topic within the first couple of sentences in your chapter will help ensure your readers have the clarity they need.

That said, sometimes you do need more 'what' content. If you are sharing a topic that is highly technical, one your readers aren't familiar with, or one where you take a different stance to most people, a little more explanation is required. You can add this explanation with definitions, examples and comparisons.

Definitions

When defining a concept, many people turn to the dictionary and paste that definition at the beginning of their chapter. While there is nothing technically wrong with this, it's a pet peeve of mine. First of all, the language of dictionary definitions is often formal and is probably completely at odds with the tone you want to strike in the rest of your writing (more on this in Part 4). Second, it doesn't add anything that you couldn't have explained in your own words. Third, it doesn't do anything for your credibility. Ultimately, it makes your chapter read like a school assignment.

Instead, your focus should be creating your own definition. If you're simply defining a term, this might be a sentence. If you're defining a broader concept, the key is to ensure you deliver it to your reader in bite-sized chunks, where you define each piece of the concept before moving on to the next one.

Let's say you wanted to explain SEO to bricks-and-mortar business owners who know nothing about online marketing. Your plain-English definition might be something like this:

- Chunk 1 – SEO stands for search engine optimisation.

- Chunk 2 – It's the art of getting your website to appear higher in Google's search results.

- Chunk 3 – There are two broad ways to achieve this – on-page optimisation and off-page optimisation.

- Chunk 4 – On-page optimisation is everything you do to your website, such as including relevant words in your content.

- Chunk 5 – Off-page optimisation is creating links on other websites that point to yours.

- Chunk 6 – Tackling both of these areas helps convince Google that you're an authority in your field, which helps your website achieve a higher rank in relevant searches.

Yes, this is quite basic for someone with a background in SEO, and you might feel like you're being too basic when you chunk down your own knowledge. The key is to start with the basic pieces, as your reader can only move on to more complex content once they have that basic understanding. In this case, now that the reader has a general idea of what you mean by SEO, they will understand what you are talking about when you start explaining why it's so important to their business and how they can start researching and incorporating keywords on their site and generating backlinks.

Examples

Have you ever tried to read the rules for a board game only to find that once you got to the end you still had no idea how to play? The reason for this is that you were trying to absorb too much at once. By contrast, after a couple of rolls of the dice, everyone's gotten the hang of it and is having fun, and the rule book falls – forgotten – behind the couch.

Some things are learnt better with a walk through, and an example is one way you can walk your reader through a complex concept. The key is to start with a familiar situation before taking your reader into unfamiliar territory, then continually revisit ideas and experiences that are familiar to your reader throughout the example.

Let's (as an example) consider the stress response from a biological perspective:

> *When the human body perceives a threat, the*
>
> *amygdala triggers a response in the hypothalamus,*
> *which activates the pituitary gland, which secretes*
> *the hormone ACTH. Meanwhile, the adrenal*
> *gland is activated and releases epinephrine. This*

> *then causes the body to produce cortisol, which leads to a range of biological responses.*

Not the most compelling read, is it? It also probably didn't help most readers understand the stress response, as most of us aren't familiar enough with the brain and hormonal systems to recognise this vocabulary.

However, nearly every modern adult has experienced the stress response at some point, and some experience it on a daily basis. Additionally, because stress is such a common problem these days, many people have some familiarity with the fight or flight response.

This means that, as a writer, you can easily link this biological explanation to your readers' existing knowledge. Consider this approach instead:

> *Have you ever been stuck in a traffic jam on the way to an important meeting? You started to sweat. Your mouth went dry. Your heart sped up. Your hands started to shake. Your brain started running through all the potential things that might go wrong.*
>
> *But have you ever wondered what might be happening inside your body?*

By starting with an experience that is relevant to your reader you make it easier for them to engage with your explanation. Then you could continue this example by running through how the stress response progresses through the body by linking the various biological responses to how your readers might experience them.

The trick is to continue asking, 'How could my readers relate to this?' throughout your explanation. In the stress response example, some of the questions a writer might ask include:

- When exactly do they start to sweat? What makes their hands start shaking?

- When do stressful events get recorded in the memory, and connected to other similar events?

- Why is it so hard to stop stressing once they have started?

- When does this response start to have an impact on their long-term health and anxiety levels?

Comparisons

Another way to explain unfamiliar concepts is to compare them to the common assumptions your readers might make. This works particularly well if you have an unusual stance on a subject that your reader is already familiar with.

An excellent example of this in practice is in Michael Gerber's *The E-Myth*. Many people use the terms 'entrepreneur' and 'business owner' interchangeably. However, in this book Gerber argues that most of the people who launch businesses aren't entrepreneurs, but are technicians who have had an entrepreneurial seizure.

Technicians are craftsmen. They are highly skilled and produce high-quality work and they equate the money they make with the amount of work they do. The issue is that most business owners can't just focus on their craft to be successful; they also need management, or organisational, skills, as well as a greater vision to guide the business into the future.

According to Gerber, entrepreneurs aren't simply business owners – entrepreneurs are the ones who hold that vision. While the technician focuses on the work itself, the entrepreneur focuses on the business as a whole and the big vision it can achieve.

The reason Gerber's definition of an entrepreneur works so well is that it is contrasted with the familiar idea of the technician or craftsman, which is the mentality most business owners have when they launch their businesses.

Action time – Expand your 'what' points

Review the body chapters in your blueprint. Which chapter topics and subtopics require 'what' content to explain concepts to your readers?

In each case, make some notes on how you might approach this.

- Is a plain-English definition the best way to get your point across? Which 'chunks' would you need to cover?

- Can the concept be explained through a familiar example? How can you keep relating the concept back to familiar experiences?

- Can you contrast your take on a concept with a commonly held belief or assumption?

In bullet points, list the points you would need to cover to explain your concept using one of these methods.

Evidence

In his bestselling book *Influence*, Robert Cialdini wrote that, 'A well-known principle of human behaviour says that when we ask someone to do us a favour we will be more successful if we provide a reason. People simply like to have reasons for what they do.'[28]

'Why' content is the reasoning behind your advice, theories and philosophies. And this reasoning is what will persuade your readers to implement your advice, believe your theories and support your philosophies.

While simply providing a reason for your argument has persuasive power,[29] adding evidence to your reasoning increases that power.[30] Case studies, interviews and quotes from experts, statistics and the findings from academic studies demonstrate that your ideas are founded on facts, prove that what you're recommending to your readers really works, and show that you are a committed author who has taken the time to do this research.

Using evidence is important for any nonfiction author, but for an entrepreneur it's essential. As you know, your book is a representation of your business. If you do it well, it creates a good impression and sets a high expectation. If you don't ... you'll struggle to see a return on your investment. By incorporating evidence, you move one step closer to creating a tool you can leverage.

---

28   Robert Cialdini, *Influence* (New York: Harper Business, 2006), 4.
29   Ellen Langer, 'The Mindlessness of Ostensibly Thoughtful Action: The Role of "Placebic" Information in Interpersonal Interaction', *Journal of Personality and Social Psychology* 36 (1978), 635–642.
30   James C. McCroskey, 'The effects of evidence in persuasive communication', *Western Speech* 31, 189–199.

So what counts as evidence, and how can you incorporate it into your book?

Case studies

Case studies, personal anecdotes and hypothetical stories are extremely compelling. By focusing on an individual journey, they are more relatable than statistics and academic studies.

They also give you a chance to explore the ramifications of someone's existing circumstances, as well as the benefits they experienced after changing, which makes case studies very effective for summarising any benefits and consequences you list.

Client case studies are not only a great way to prove a point but also help boost your credibility by showing that your business and the service you provide *works*.

Meanwhile, personal anecdotes allow you to gently showcase your experience and make a more personal connection with your reader. Hypothetical examples can explain a situation or concept when you either don't have a client story or a personal story that will fit, or you feel that going into a real story will be overly complex.

Regardless of the type of story you share, the format is the same, and should cover the following areas:

- The person's original situation – where were they before they followed your advice, and what were the negative aspects of this situation?

- What prompted them to change – this is optional, but can work quite well. Think about what catalysed their change. What was the straw that broke the camel's back?

- What they did – how did they implement your advice? Or, if you helped them with something, what did you do?

- Their experience – again, this is optional. However, going through their experience of the change can sometimes be helpful when it comes to difficult or unusual circumstances.

- The results – what benefits did they experience as a result of taking these actions?

Action time – Add case studies to your blueprint

For each of the chapter topics and subtopics in your blueprint, think of a case study, anecdote or hypothetical story you could use to demonstrate why your argument is important.

In your plan, make a note of the person in the example or case study and the main points you need to cover, including:

- Their original situation
- What prompted them to change
- What they did
- Their experience
- The results

Expert interviews

Interviews allow you to incorporate the thoughts of industry experts in your book and are a great way to build your content if you already have some people in mind who have knowledge to share and the willingness to share it.

Interviews are credibility pieces – by including the thoughts of an expert, their expert status rubs off on you. Whether or not they actually endorse you in the process, on a subconscious level the reader often interprets this as the expert's seal of approval, which further cements your own expert status.

Now it's easy to get stumped on this one and think, 'Well *I* don't know any experts,' but you might be surprised.

An expert is anyone who knows more than your target readers (having a fancy job title also helps). So this means anyone you know who works in your field counts as an expert. If you're writing about property investing, then experts could include mortgage brokers, financial planners, real estate agents or property developers. If you're writing a book about online marketing, then your experts could include bloggers, information product developers, social media marketers and web designers.

How to approach your list of experts

Once you have a list of potential experts, how do you approach them?

Hopefully you'll know them personally, in which case an email or phone call will do. If not, the next best thing is to find a mutual contact who can introduce you. The best way to do this is to search for the expert on LinkedIn or Facebook, and then look at their connections or friends. As you go through the list, see who your mutual contacts are. If you have a good relationship with one of their contacts, send them a message asking them to introduce you to the expert. This helps break the ice and means they're more likely to be receptive to your request.

If you can't find a mutual connection, then you can always try approaching an expert through their website. They might welcome the publicity and the opportunity to say they were quoted in your book, particularly if they haven't been quoted before. A side benefit is that they might then be willing to help you promote your book.

What to ask

When interviewing someone, whether doing it over the phone, in person or by email, stick to a few key questions. This is particularly important when it comes to email. Remember that experts are busy people. If they see a list of ten questions they're likely to feel that it's too much work and put it off until they have more time. And, as we all know, we very rarely have more time at some magical point in the future.

Instead, think about four or five questions that are directly related to the topic or issue you want them to comment on. Focus on the information that will be most relevant to your readers and that will best prove your point.

Some common question categories include:

- The most common mistakes people make concerning your topic,

- The major problems your target readers are experiencing,

- The best way to solve these problems, and

- Case studies from their clients and network.

It's important to include some credibility markers when you refer to experts in your book. However, because you only have four or five questions, I don't recommend asking about this in your interview – you can find out about their background on their website or LinkedIn.

When it comes to giving the biography of the interviewee, remember that less is more – if you write about them for a page or two, your readers are likely to lose interest. Your readers are reading to either solve their problems or fulfil their desires, so if you prevent them from reaching the practical information that will help them do that it can quickly become frustrating. Instead, focus on a sentence or two that includes the interviewee's name and some credibility markers such as their company, the number of clients they've worked with, and any books or other publications they've written.

Action time – Add interviews to your blueprint

Go through your blueprint and think about who in your network could be interviewed as an expert on your chapter topics or subtopics.

Write their names in the relevant area, as well as four or five questions you would like to ask them, such as:

- The most common mistakes your target readers make concerning your topic,

- The major problems your target readers are experiencing – focus on general information about your target readers, such as statistics based on the people your interviewee works with,

- The best way to solve these problems – again, focus on which methods your interviewee has seen get the best results based on their experience, and

- Case studies from their clients and network.

Then, email or phone them to organise the interview!

Statistics and academic studies

Depending on your area of expertise, statistics and academic studies might be relevant to your book.

Statistics can work very well to quickly make a point that may otherwise take a paragraph or two to explain. Likewise, academic studies have a higher level of credibility than client case studies, simply because they involve more people. This makes them more reliable than a case study that might have been a one-off.

However, there are two disadvantages to using these forms of evidence. The first is that they are highly impersonal and technical, which can make your reader tune out if you use them excessively.[31]

The second issue is that, unless you already have a range of studies and statistics on hand, it can be difficult to find relevant ones. As a result, if you get attached to including a statistic or study relating to a certain point, searching for one could set you back days or even weeks.

Action time – Add statistics and studies to your blueprint

Go through your blueprint again and find any topics where you already know about or have access to relevant academic studies and statistics. If you do, make a note with the source.

So my thoughts are, if you already happen to have a library of statistics and case studies ready to use (for example, you might be a part of an academic community or still have your books and resources from when you qualified), they can be a great asset for your book. If you don't, then don't stress – consider them an optional extra. As long as you have other forms of evidence, not including these won't damage your credibility.

---

31   What's excessive? In a 30,000-word book, if you're averaging more than a couple of studies or statistics per chapter, that's probably too much. If you happen to have one chapter where a number of different studies are relevant, that's okay – just ease up on the next one.

Exercises

If you are writing a how-to or list book, you also need 'how' content. This is where the real value lies for your readers, as they won't achieve the results you promise without being able to take action on your advice.

So what is 'how' content? In some cases, the subtopics in your chapter may be enough to act as 'how' content, such as if you give your readers five key ideas to consider in a certain area. If you want to make this even more tangible, I recommend including questions, activities and action items.

Questions encourage your readers to reflect on what they have learnt and consider how they might integrate your lessons into their lives. They are valuable when you share a concept that doesn't require your readers to complete a task but where you still want them to pause and reflect on the importance of what you have shared before moving on.

These questions can simply be listed as bullet points within your chapter, with the instruction for your reader to take some time (the more specific, the better; if you want them to spend five to ten minutes on the questions, then say so) to either think about the question, or to write down their answers in a journal or workbook.

Activities include templates, worksheets and multi-step tasks. These help your readers learn new concepts, as well as complete essential steps of your process before moving on to the next topic or step in your book. They are useful for inciting action in more complex areas of your book, or areas that they might find unfamiliar.

A great example of this is in *Navigating Career Crossroads* by Jane Jackson, which helps readers bounce back after redundancy and find their next position. A common piece of job-searching advice is to network, but for those who have never networked to find a position before, this advice can feel vague and overwhelming. In one of her chapters, Jane outlines a five-step networking process where each step features mini-activities. Some of these include a template for listing the details of your contacts, steps for delivering your pitch and getting feedback from friends and family, and steps on delivering your pitch and following up with key decision makers at companies of interest.

Activities often work well for coaches and other professionals who work with clients one-on-one – by guiding your readers through each step of an activity you do with your clients in person or over the phone, they get a taste of what it might be like to work with you. An added bonus is that, if you already use such activities in your work, it means you don't need to create new ones for your book – simply copy and paste your existing worksheets and instructions into your blueprint!

Finally, action items are a good way to give your readers tangible steps to implement when a longer activity isn't necessary. This might be because you've already outlined the larger activity earlier in your book, and simply want to give your reader a reminder to do it, or it might be because the piece of advice isn't that complex so doesn't require a detailed activity.

Action time – Expand your 'how' points

If you are writing a list book or how-to book, look for the 'how' section in each of your subtopics. What can you add to make your advice more tangible and actionable?

Think about:

- Thinking questions – is this a concept you'd like your readers to reflect on? If so, list some questions that would help with this reflection. In each case, aim for at least three questions and no more than ten.

- Activities – is the task you want your readers to perform more complex, requiring templates, worksheets or multi-step actions? If so, share an activity. If it is a book-specific activity, briefly list the steps you will need to cover. If you already have resources for this activity, copy and paste them into your blueprint.

- Action items – is there a single, simple action your readers can take to implement your advice? Or do you just want to remind your readers that they need to take action? Make a note of the action.

Thud or dud?

Content is the difference between a credible book that is valued by clients, partners and the media, and a free booklet or brochure that's likely to be discarded as marketing material. Content is the difference between standing out in your industry and blending into the crowd. Content is the difference between being an author-ity and being a wannabe.

However, while explanation, evidence and exercises will flesh out the outline you created in Chapters 5 and 6, there's one more secret ingredient that will take your book from being interesting and useful to being memorable and shareable. That ingredient is engagement.

Bonus resource

Want to short-cut your writing process? Head over to grammarfactory.com/bb-bonus to find out how you can recycle your existing content to bulk up your book.

CHAPTER 8

The cherry on top – engagement

Once upon a time, a university professor divided his students into groups of five or six and gave each group a research project. One group was asked how they could improve the jury deliberation process and was required to present their findings to a local district judge at the end of the semester.

So they got to work – they interviewed the judges in the jurisdiction, they interviewed the plaintiffs and defendants, they interviewed the prosecuting attorneys and defence attorneys, and they interviewed people who had served as jurors.

They asked the questions you'd expect – which trial did you serve on? How long did it last? What sort of information could you have in the jury room? Did you get instructions? How long did you need to work? Did you get snacks?

At the end of the semester, they concluded that none of these things mattered. Instead, the only consistent element that made a difference was the shape of the table in the jury room. In jury rooms with rectangular tables, the person at the head of the table (whether the foreperson or not) ended up dominating the conversation, resulting in a less robust debate. In jury rooms with round tables, a more egalitarian debate ensued, and the jurors felt like a better verdict was delivered.

With this finding, the students were excited to make their big presentation to the judge at the end of their project. The judge was equally excited by their discovery and made a decree: 'In all the courthouses in my jurisdiction, get rid of any round tables. I want rectangular tables from now on.'

Unlike the students, who were excited about changing the world for the better, the judge wasn't interested in a more accurate or just process – he wanted a faster one to reduce his backlog.[32]

Now imagine if you were one of those students – an idealistic twenty-something who thought this was going to be your chance to change the world for the better and, in the end, you did the exact opposite.

Jayson Zoller, Director of Consumer and Communications Research at Procter and Gamble, has been telling this story for twenty years to make a single point…

You need to be clear about your objectives before you start anything. If you only figure them out partway through, more often than not you'll be disappointed by the end result.

How many times have you been hooked on a good story? Have you ever stayed up late to read a novel you couldn't put down, or to finish a movie you couldn't turn

---

32   Paul Smith, *Lead with a Story* (New York: AMACON, 2012), 1–2.

off? Have you been motivated by another entrepreneur's success, or moved to support a cause that you read about in the paper?

Storytelling has become very important in the business arena, and many of the world's most successful companies use storytelling as a leadership tool, including Apple, Microsoft, Nike, Xerox, Motorola, 3M, Kodak, Disney, Costco, FedEx, Saatchi & Saatchi and NASA.[33]

Why?

Because stories create an emotional connection with their readers, listeners and viewers. This emotional connection makes it easier to share information, builds rapport, fosters trust and creates memories. According to Jennifer Aaker of Stanford University, stories are up to twenty-two times more memorable than facts alone.[34]

For an entrepreneur, though, what's most relevant is how stories can influence behaviour, changing the way we think, feel and act. This can engage a team, transform a negative situation into a positive one, and help convince a potential client to buy.

According to psychologists Melanie Green and Tim Brock, entering the world of a story transforms the way we process information. Because humans naturally want to work through stories, we quickly become absorbed. And the more absorbed we are, the more power a story has to change us.[35]

---

33   Paul Smith, *Lead with a Story* (New York: AMACON, 2012), 3.
34   Jennifer Aaker, 'Harnessing the Power of Stories', *Lean in*, accessed November 4, 2014, http://leanin.org/education/harnessing-the-power-of-stories/
35   Timothy C. Brock & Melanie C. Green, 'The Role of Transportation in the Persuasiveness of Public Narratives', *Journal of Personality and Social Psychology* 79 (2000): 701–721, Accessed November 4, 2014, doi: 10.1037//0022-3514.79.5.701.

When we are absorbed in a story we lower our defences. This makes stories more effective than pure facts and evidence on every level.

However, while entrepreneurs are cottoning on to the value of storytelling, it's difficult to get right. Just as having a Facebook account doesn't make you a social media expert, simply knowing that storytelling is important doesn't mean you have the tools to tell a great story.

So how do you tell a great story?

Know your audience

Just as you need to know your audience to write a great book, you need to know your audience to tell a great story. If you don't, your readers will tune out.

Now I'm going to assume that your target readers are your potential clients and that, being an entrepreneur who has already spent significant time thinking about your business, you already know who these people are. If you aren't sure, revisit the reader test in Chapter 1.

So how can you create a story that's tailored to these readers?

The best way is to start with a situation that they can relate to. If your readers are mums who are also entrepreneurs, you might start with a story where the mum is at her son's soccer match and is checking emails on her iPhone. She hears cheering and suddenly her son runs up to ask if she saw his goal, and she realises she missed it.

Or if your readers are struggling start-ups, you might start with the scenario where business starts going really well for a couple of months, the entrepreneur is swamped with client work so stops marketing, and then the work calms down and there are no new leads so the entrepreneur needs to start marketing again, only to repeat the cycle.

If you aren't sure what your readers might relate to, you have two options. The first is to simply reach out to people who are your target readers and ask them. If this isn't an option, then you can fall back on more universal experiences across our culture, such as little frustrations like waiting in line when you're in a rush, being stuck in traffic, or getting the wrong meal at a restaurant and wondering whether or not to send it back. The goal is to start in a way that immediately connects with your readers. Because, once they are hooked, you can take them anywhere you want to go.

> ### Action time – Connect with your readers
>
> List some situations your target readers will relate to that you can work into your stories.

Know your objective

The second key to telling a great story is knowing your objective. Unfortunately, many entrepreneurs only tell stories for the sake of telling them. While this can create some interest or engagement, if your story doesn't have a purpose, you aren't going to get the results you want.

What do you want to achieve with your stories? Do you want to share a personal lesson so that your reader has a better understanding of your beliefs and values? Do you want to be vulnerable to help build trust? Do you want to make your readers uncomfortable enough to consider a different point of view? Do you want to persuade them?

Most stories fall into one of four categories.

The first is stories that engage or connect with your readers. These stories make your reader want to keep reading – they feel like they can't put your book down because they have to know what happens next. These stories also work as a form of credit, where even if your readers encounter part of your book that's challenging or a bit dry, they will persist because of the engagement you built up earlier.

The second category is stories that prove a point, such as the examples and case studies you use to bolster your 'why' content. As discussed in the previous chapter, providing evidence for your reasoning makes it more powerful, which means your readers are more likely to subscribe to your views.

The third category is stories that teach a lesson, or have a moral. These stories often work well when the lesson you want to teach is one where your readers might feel like they've heard it all before – bringing the lesson to life in a story helps remind your readers of the importance of the lesson. The story that opened this chapter is a good example of this in practice, where the lesson was for listeners to be clear on their objectives before starting any project.

The final category is stories that explain a concept. One of the best examples I've seen of this is a piece titled *My Half-Baked Bubble*, written by Joshuah Bearman.[36] Published by the *New York Times* at the height of the Global Financial Crisis, this story explains how market bubbles burst through the analogy of a schoolyard marketplace where, every lunchtime, his classmates would trade their sweets. Unfortunately for Joshua, his 'was a Spartan household: no chocolate, cookies or extraneous sugar. For [them], Rice Krispies cereal was supposed to be some kind of special indulgence.' As a result, his lunches had no value in the marketplace.

So what did he do? He invented an investment opportunity – an incredible cake that his mum would bake at the end of the year for all of his friends. If his classmates wanted in, they would need to invest with their cupcakes, chips and chocolate bars. As more and more people bought into this cake the bubble grew … until the only way this cake could pay back his debts was if it defied the laws of physics. Eventually a classmate blew the whistle, the bubble burst, the old economy rebuilt itself, and he was an outsider once more.

---

36   Joshuah Bearman, 'My Half-Baked Bubble', *New York Times*, December 19, 2009, accessed April 14, 2015, http://www.nytimes.com/2009/12/20/opinion/20bearman.html

---

Action time – Get clear on your objective

For every story you consider adding into your book, get clear on your objective. Do you want to:

- Engage,
- Prove your point,
- Teach a lesson, or
- Explain a concept?

Having a clear objective will influence which stories you keep and which you cut, where you put them in your chapters, and how you tell them.

Craft your plot

Have you ever tried to retell a joke? You start with the premise, go through what you can remember of the narrative, suddenly remember something that you should have included earlier, and then somehow end up at the punch line but it doesn't land the way it should.

And then what happens? You say, 'I guess you had to be there.'

Like your book and your chapters, each story needs a clear structure to create an emotional connection with your readers. If you don't have a structure, your attempt at storytelling will simply be a list of facts and won't create the engagement that makes stories powerful.

How do you craft a great plot? By following a dramatic arc.

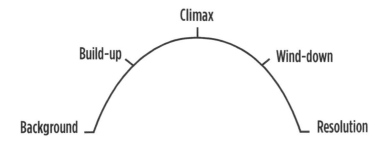

This arc covers five stages:

1. *Background* – This is the 'before' state, which introduces information about the characters, the setting and more. It is how your hero has arrived where they are today.

2. *Build-up* – This is a series of events that build towards the climax.

3. *Climax* – This is the turning point in the story, the catalyst that changes the hero's fate.

4. *Wind-down* – Here the conflict unravels and the hero starts to triumph over the villain. Keep in mind that your villain doesn't need to be another character – it can be a situation such as a business or health struggle, or even the hero fighting against himself, such as battling his desire to give up.

5. *Resolution* – The conflict is resolved and the world in your story finds balance again. If you have a lesson to share, this is where you share it.

What does this look like in action? In Gareth Brock's book *Have Pet, Will Travel*, the story of how he adopted his dog, Ebony, follows this five-part structure.

1. *Background* – 'My Ebony was born as a result of an international stopover. Her mother, a champion Parson Russell Terrier, was on her way from South Africa to New Zealand to attend a dog show.'

2. *Build-up* – 'At her layover in Sydney, she escaped from the airport and was on the run for fifteen days.'

3. *Climax* – 'While on the run, she found herself an Aussie boyfriend (suspected to be a German Shepherd), got herself pregnant and was then hit by a car!'

4. *Wind-down* – 'Thankfully, she survived the accident (which incidentally made Page 2 of the *Sydney Morning Herald*), and ended up at my sister's veterinary practice needing to be nursed through her pregnancy due to her broken legs.'

5. *Resolution* – 'Ebony, a little black and tan fluff ball with white socks, was born just before Christmas, and the rest is history. With this in mind, and as a frequent traveller, I have always been cautious when it comes to travelling by plane with Ebony so we don't have a repeat of the same incident.'[37]

---

37   Gareth Brock, *Have Pet, Will Travel: The Essential Guide for Travelling Pet Owners* (Sydney: Pet Check-in, 2014), 75–76.

Depending on the length of your story, you might not use all five parts (I recommend focusing on the climax and surrounding action, as these are usually the most engaging parts of a story). However, it is useful to consider all of them in the creation process before cutting back.

Action time – Craft your plot

Try out this five-act structure on your stories. Where are each of the five parts? Is there a clear climax? Do you spend a long time on the background and results of a story, or is it action oriented?

Use these questions to guide your storytelling.

Test your story

There's one more step to create a winning story. Like hiring someone who doesn't live up to their résumé, many stories look great on paper but don't have the impact you want. Unfortunately many entrepreneurs take their stories straight to the public, without testing and tweaking them first.

So, once you're clear on your readers, your objectives and your structure, test it. Share it with everyone you can, particularly people who are your ideal readers, and gauge their reactions. Do they get it? Were they engaged? What worked and what didn't? Can they tell it back to you? What did they remember?

Remember to share the written version as well as sharing it verbally – things that work in conversation don't always have the same impact in writing.

Action time – Test your stories

Test your stories. Observe your listeners:

- Are they engaged?
- Does their attention wander?
- Do they look like they're following the story?
- Are the bits you thought were the most powerful having the expected impact?

Then ask them:

- Did they get it?
- What did they like? What didn't they like?
- Can they tell it back to you?
- What do they remember?

Use this feedback to tweak your stories.

Where to include stories in your book

So now that you know the benefits of storytelling and how to craft a great one, where can you incorporate stories in your book? This depends on your objective.

If you want to share some of your story to allow your readers to get to know you, the introduction is a good location. Including the relevant parts of your story in the introduction helps answer the question, 'Why are you the best person to be writing about this subject?'

If you want to engage with your readers, add stories to the beginning of your chapters to draw them in.

If your story is designed to explain a concept or to demonstrate what your readers should (and shouldn't) do, they can work well in your 'what' content as a way of introducing that concept.

Finally, if you want to prove a point, include the story in your 'why' content as a form of evidence – this is where examples and case studies can work really well, not only as a form of evidence, but also as a way to engage.

Action time – Weave stories into your blueprint

Look at your blueprint. Where could you incorporate some stories? Consider:

- Chapter beginnings – do you have a story that is related to your chapter topic?

- To prove a point – which points would best be proved with a story? Look at the 'why' arguments you make in each chapter, as well as the 'how' exercises, which could benefit from a story about how the exercise works in practice.

> - To get to know you – which personal stories can you share that are related to your content and provide value to the reader?
>
> In each case, add some notes about the story to the relevant part of your blueprint. Include:
>
> - How it relates to the reader
> - Your objective
> - Each step in the five-part structure

You can also include personal anecdotes throughout the book, where relevant. The main thing to keep in mind is that your book isn't about you – it's about your readers, so keep the focus on them.

The payoff

Imagine that you are at an industry event, standing behind a table covered with stacks of your book. You sell copies, sign pages, shake hands and smile. Things are going well.

You notice someone hanging around the edges of the crowd. They look slightly awkward, as if they're in the wrong place. As the crowd dies down they approach the table.

'I already have a copy of your book, and I just wanted to tell you how much I loved it.'

You smile. 'Thank you. What did you like about it?' You expect them to rattle off how valuable they found your advice, or how your framework made them look at their situation in a new light.

Instead they say, 'The thing that really got me was the story you shared about...' and launch into the story itself. You're surprised at how much detail they remember, and even more surprised when they say, 'I couldn't stop telling people about it – there are probably another ten or twenty people who bought your book because of me!'

No matter how strong your explanation, evidence and exercises are, your stories are what will make your book live on in the hearts and minds of your readers.

CONTENT WORKSHEET

1. Go through your blueprint and, based on your existing knowledge, add more notes to cover the points you've listed in more detail.

   - 'What' content – how can you explain a complex topic with definitions, examples or comparisons to common assumptions?
   - 'Why' content – what evidence can you add to explain the risks and benefits you list in more detail?
   - 'How' content – do you have any existing exercises you go through with your clients?

2. Focus on your evidence, or 'why' content, adding the following information to your blueprint:

   - Case studies/anecdotes/stories – aim for one for each chapter and include:
     - The person's original situation
     - What prompted them to change
     - What they did
     - Their experience
     - The results

- Interviews with experts – focus on including these where relevant. Stick to four or five questions and think about the following areas:

  o The most common mistakes your target readers make concerning your topic

  o The major problems your target readers are experiencing

  o The best way to solve these problems

  o Case studies from their clients and network

- Statistics and academic studies – focus on areas where you already know about or have access to this information; don't start looking for this information from scratch.

3. Where could you incorporate some stories?

- Chapter beginnings – do you have a story that is related to your chapter topic?

- To prove a point – which points would best be proved with a story?

- To teach – are there any complex topics you discuss that could be explained with a story?

- To get to know you – which personal stories can you share that are related to your content and provide value to the reader?

4. Add detail to each story, including:

   - How it relates to the reader

   - Your objective

   - Each step in the five-part structure:
     - Backround
     - Build-up
     - Climax
     - Wind-down
     - Resolution

5. Review your existing content, including your website, brochures, blog posts, articles, case studies, interviews and client worksheets. Do you already have content that addresses the above areas?

   - Collect whatever is related to your book topic.

   - Organise this content – what fits where? What would fit in your introduction, your body chapters and your conclusion? Copy this content and paste it under the relevant bullet points in your blueprint.

PART 4

THE RIGHT LANGUAGE

CHAPTER 9

Wordsmith your work

Language matters.

Now I'm a writer, so of course I'm going to say that. Working with language is my job, and you'd expect me to wax lyrical on the merits of the dash over the semicolon, the importance of cutting a slogan from five words to three, and my preference for plain English over technical jargon for hours on end.

But this book isn't about me – it's about you.

And language matters for you, too.

In a face-to-face transaction, a salesman speaks directly to his potential customer. He might start with a handshake, make some small talk, and then go into his spiel.

If you were the customer you would be making unconscious judgements about whether he is really getting you a good deal or whether he is trying to milk you for all you're worth by observing his clothes, his body language, his sales pitch and more.

Interestingly, words only make up seven per cent of your evaluation. The other ninety-three per cent is made up of body language and paralinguistic cues, such as his volume, pitch, range and speed.

Fifty-five per cent of your assessment is based on body language – you're using his stance, his gestures and his expressions to determine what kind of a person he is and whether or not you want to hand over your credit card.

However, once visuals are removed, you have fewer clues to make that judgement, making the forty-five per cent of communication that is verbal more important.[38]

The bulk of that verbal communication is made up of paralinguistic cues like volume and pitch. But once the voice is taken away, you only have that final seven per cent to go off – the words he's using.

So while you might be able to easily win over a potential client or partner in person, your body language and voice play a large role in your potential client's or partner's decision. In your book they don't have these clues … which makes your words much more important.

So prepare for a grammar lesson! (Cue maniacal laugh.)

Just kidding – I'm not going to torture you in that special way.

While having correct spelling, grammar and punctuation are important from a credibility perspective,

---

38   These percentages are based on communications studies that Professor Albert Mehrabian and colleagues at the University of California, Los Angeles performed in the 1960s, the results of which were published in his book *Silent Messages* in 1971. While the exact percentages are debated today, most experts agree with the general premise that, while verbal communication is important, the majority of our communication is nonverbal.

I don't think you need to be a linguist or grammarian to write a great book. In fact, spelling and grammar is one of the easiest things to outsource.

The two elements that are more difficult to outsource are explaining your area of expertise in plain English, and incorporating your personality into your writing.

The power of plain English

I recently read an article on *The New Yorker* website where journalist John Lanchester discussed the annual flooding of the Nile in ancient Egypt.[39]

According to Lanchester, the calendar was divided into three seasons. These seasons were linked with the river and the agricultural cycle it determined: inundation, growth and harvest. The harvest was dependent on the size of the flood – if there was too little water there would be famine, if there was too much it would destroy the surrounding villages, but if it was just right then Egypt would prosper.

Each year priests would perform complicated rituals to predict the coming floods and that year's harvest. The rituals included unfamiliar symbols based on mythology, making it impossible for anyone outside the religious elite to make similar predictions, and they used this knowledge to remain in power for thousands of years.

---

39   John Lanchester, 'Money Talks', *The New Yorker*, August 4, 2014, accessed October 30, 2014, http://www.newyorker.com/magazine/2014/08/04/money-talks-6

However, what the average Egyptian didn't realise was that the priests were cheating. The priests were using Nilometers – structures designed to measure the Nile's water level during the flood season – which were situated in temples that only the priests and rulers could access. Combined with centuries of accurate records of flood patterns, this elite could make very accurate predictions about each year's floods, and the rituals presented to the public played a very small part in this.

As Lanchester wrote, 'The world is full of priesthoods.' Today these priesthoods consist of professionals who use complicated, high-brow and technical language to maintain the mystique of their knowledge.

In the legal arena you find phrases like, 'Any reference to a specific statute include any statutory extension or modification amendment or re-enactment of such statute and any regulations or orders made under such statute and any general reference to "statute" or "statutes" include any regulations or orders made under such statute or statutes.'[40]

In job advertisements you find language like, 'Procurement is targeted with delivering savings on generic goods and services pan-BBC through a competitive management initiative and driving compliance. The Category Manager Logistics Ground Transport is responsible to the Head of Production and

---

40 'Harrow Road Meeting Room Terms & Conditions of Hire', accessed October 30, 2014, https://www.cityoflondon.gov.uk/things-to-do/green-spaces/epping-forest/sports-events-and-activities/Documents/wfpf-meeting-room-terms-and-conditions.pdf

Logistics and Senior Category Manager Logistics.' Can you guess the position?[41]

Meanwhile, in any marketing team you'll hear terms like TVC, PIR, above-the-fold, backlinking and clickbait thrown around in their weekly WIP.

And when it comes to finance, a 2010 survey from Consumer Focus Wales found that sixty-five per cent of people found the language used by banks and other financial service providers confusing, with twenty-eight per cent admitting to paying for services without understanding what they were paying for.[42]

Why does this happen?

Part of it is because the concepts this language represents are complex. In legalese, there's also the need to avoid uncertainty and ambiguity with accurate language. In politics or when giving bad news, people use formal language to distance themselves from the message, soften it or even cover it up.

But most of the time, it comes down to wanting to make a distinction between 'us' (the experts) and 'them' (everyone else).

This is why new entrepreneurs' websites commonly use fancy words and obscure technical terms. After all, what better way is there to demonstrate your education and your experience? What better way is there to prove that you're the real deal?

---

41   This was a job ad for someone to book taxis for BBC executives. Source: Fry's *Planet Word*

42   'Consumer watchdog criticises banks' confusing jargon,' *Wales Online*, July 26, 2010, accessed October 30, 2014, http://www.walesonline.co.uk/news/wales-news/consumer-watchdog-criticises-banks-confusing-1909802

Then there's always the fear that, if you don't use formal and complex language, a potential client might find out that you aren't as big or experienced as you claim. And then they might choose to work with someone else.

Whether you've been in business for a month, a year, five years or fifteen years, these concerns still come up. And while you might have become more at peace with your website and marketing over time, I've noticed that these fears seem to bubble to the surface again when writing a book, simply because it's unfamiliar territory. So authors become more formal. They insert longer words, technical language and academic phrases into their writing to make themselves sound more knowledgeable, more authoritative, and more credible.

However, I have a secret. If you are confident in yourself and your message, you don't need to use language to demonstrate your authority. Fancy, formal or technical language doesn't equal credibility. Fancy, formal and technical language can actually *put off* the very readers you want to pull in.

Today, readers have more choices than ever. There are trillions of gigabytes of information available online. Full-length books can be delivered wirelessly to your iPad or Kindle in seconds. Hard-copy books can be sent from the other side of the world in a couple of weeks, with free postage to boot. So if you're making it difficult for readers to digest the information in your book, why should they keep reading when they could easily access similar information elsewhere?

Complex, technical language doesn't win credibility – it loses readers.

Plain English, short sentences, and simple words are what readers crave. By contrast, buzz-words, jargon and corporate speak are becoming so overused that the general public are tuning them out.

This isn't the corporate world where you're expected to fill reports with jargon to make it sound like you know what you're talking about, ward off questions or impress someone higher up. This is entrepreneurship. Your credibility comes from your knowledge, the value you add and the ideas you share. You can use simple language because you actually know what you're talking about. You want to invite questions and start conversations with potential clients, partners and the media. And, to be honest, when you publish your book, you really don't need to worry about impressing anyone. The proof is in the paperback.

And if you're still not convinced, take a moment to think about the Albert Einstein quote, 'If you can't explain it simply, you don't understand it well enough.'

Now while a good editor will help you with this, it also helps if you start your book with the intention of keeping it conversational (remember, your editor is probably not an expert in your field, and if you get too technical she may struggle to understand your writing just as much as your target readers will).

So how do you do it?

Here are a few tips for you to keep in mind as you sit down to write:

- Omit needless words! It's far better to have 20,000 words that get straight to the point than 40,000 words of waffle.

- Never use a long word when a short one will do.

- Avoid the passive voice – phrases like 'the following results were achieved' feel overly formal and academic. Who achieved the result? You? A client? Your team? Then say so! 'We achieved the following results' is far more engaging.

- Use contractions liberally – writing common contractions like 'don't', 'isn't', 'it's' and 'can't' in full can make your writing feel very formal.

- Write like you talk – if you wouldn't say something, don't write it.

- Refer to yourself as 'I' (or 'we', if you're co-authoring your book) and your reader as 'you' – your reader should feel like they are having a conversation with you.

- Try reading your work to a twelve-year-old – if they don't understand it, it's time to go back to your laptop.

Action time – Eliminate dreary corporate speak

Think about the conversations you frequently have with your ideal readers. This might include the conversation when you pitch to new clients, when you review your progress with existing clients, or when you're introduced to a potential client at a networking event.

When do they lose interest? When do they stop asking questions, start to glaze over, or start discreetly looking for someone else to talk to? Pay attention to this moment – there's a good chance you've fallen into using technical jargon.

Instead, think of how you'd explain those concepts to a twelve-year-old – this is the same way you should explain them in your book.

The power of personality

While your editor can help with keeping things conversational, an area that's impossible to outsource is bringing your personality into your writing.

A common objection that comes up for entrepreneurs thinking about writing a book is, 'But there are already so many books on money management/personal development/diet/exercise/marketing/crystal-ball gazing/[insert your profession here].'

You know what? You're right – there *are* a lot of books on your subject. In fact, there are already a lot of books out there on how to write a book, but here you are reading mine. Why? Assuming you're not my mum, there was probably something about my personality that came through, either in my marketing, in a sample you downloaded, or when we met in person.

This is what sets this book apart from every other book-writing book out there – my personality. And your personality is what will set your book apart from every other book in your industry. While there are many other entrepreneurs in your field, and many of them may offer similar advice, you are the only *you* in your field, and the language you use in your book is how you leverage that part of you.

How can I be so sure? Because many of the books I edit are written about similar industries, and no two books have been alike.

Let's take a moment to think about a common piece of financial planning advice: managing credit card debt. Not the most scintillating topic, is it? Some might even say it's a bit dull, and it's definitely nowhere near as sexy as billion-dollar investments.

Yet look at how the following author raised the issue of credit card debt.

> *Rule #6 – Credit cards are evil minions*
>
> *Once again, you might feel I've gone too far. 'Evil minions? Really?'*
>
> *Well, in looking for an appropriate analogy for the destructive force credit cards have on many*

people's lives, I only had to go as far as one of my favourite movies – Despicable Me 2.

One of the baddies finds that if he takes one of the yellow minions (who are completely loyal to the lead character Gru, even if they do sometimes create more chaos than they actually help), and adds his special purple serum that they turn into ... 'an indestructible, mindless, killing machine!'

And that is pretty much how I feel about credit cards.

Indestructible ... yup.

Mindless ... seems so.

Killing machine ... well they frequently kill any possibility of getting ahead financially.[43]

This extract is from Peita Diamantidis's book *Finance Action Hero*, which teaches regular people how to tackle their finances like action heroes. Every chapter features quotes from action movies and there are references to heroes, villains, miraculous feats and super powers throughout.

This angle sets her book apart from all the other financial planning books out there. However, this angle wouldn't have worked if Peita didn't genuinely adore her adventure movies and characters, and it's only because

---

43   Peita Diamantidis, *Finance Action Hero* (North Sydney: DeltaPlan Holdings Pty Ltd, 2014), 113–114.

she brought this genuine interest to her writing that her sense of humour and fun comes through.

This is the key to injecting personality into your writing – it has to be your *real* personality. Peita didn't put on a fake personality to make her book different. She has a rather silly sense of humour and is full of laughs and fun and exclamation marks, whether you're reading her book, talking to her on the phone, or reading her Facebook posts. This is why it worked.

If she had just assumed this personality for her book, on the other hand, it could have resulted in potential clients calling her financial planning practice only to discover that she and her team were not like that at all in real life.

Inconsistency is one of the dangers of having so many different ways to communicate today. And while you may not realise it, inconsistent communication costs you clients.

If we return to the salesman from the beginning of this chapter, he was making a pitch directly to his potential customer. The conversation might have ranged from a few minutes to a few hours, and the entire time he would have had the same haircut, been wearing the same suit, and been speaking in the same tone. It's unlikely, in a regular sales conversation, that he would have suddenly started shouting, jumping up and down, or turning away and blushing.

What most entrepreneurs don't realise is that they are doing this to their clients every single day.

When it comes to running a business these days, things are a little different. What used to be a single, face-to-face sales conversation can now take place over several weeks or months. And it's no longer face-to-face; it's via Facebook, Twitter, your website, your blog, email, newsletters, videos, teleseminars, podcasts, over the phone/Skype, in person *and* through your book.

If you're like most modern entrepreneurs, you are probably communicating via several of these mediums, and many of your followers may be subscribed to all of them. So if the way you communicate in your book is different to how you sound on a podcast, they'll know.

If you communicate differently, it unsettles them. It makes them feel like something's a little bit off. They don't know which voice is the real you, and this can raise their defences.

And then they don't want to buy from you.

I once saw this in practice in a Facebook group for entrepreneurs. I was doing a business course where we were asked to post a number of videos in the group. One of the women couldn't post a video due to technical difficulties, so she did a regular post instead.

She used capital letters, exclamation marks, emoticons and said LOL, which made her seem almost aggressively enthusiastic, yet somehow endearing at the same time. She seemed so excited, and I was excited for her and everything she was sharing. Over the next few weeks she was very active in the group, and always wrote in the same tone: aggressive enthusiasm.

Then she finally posted the video.

On the video she was sweet, quiet and unassuming. In fact, her personality was so unlike the one she had conveyed through her written posts that it seemed like the person on the video was a different person to the one I had been getting to know over the previous weeks.

On an intellectual level, I know that there are some mediums where we're less comfortable than others and that our tone can change with our mood and our energy, but on an emotional level I felt like our connection had shattered. I didn't know which personality was the real her, and when I'd previously been very curious about her work, now I didn't feel like I wanted to work with her anymore.

All because of one video.

Your book has the same impact (as does all of the marketing connected to your book). If something's off, the connection you've been building with your readers can be destroyed in an instant. Ultimately, your book needs to be a consistent representation of you. To achieve that, it needs to be true to your personality.

Action time – Uncover your personality

To incorporate your personality into your writing, you need to be clear on both your personality and how you express that personality. Because we tend to take our own unique personality traits for granted, I recommend asking your clients, colleagues, friends and family the following questions:

- How would they describe you to someone else?

- What makes you different to everyone else they know?

- Why do they like working with you?

Write down the qualities that they share – they might be qualified, measured, enthusiastic, fun, lovely, friendly, encouraging, informative, approachable or something else.

The next step is figuring out how to incorporate these qualities into your writing.

Once again, turn to your network. Ask them:

- Why do they think you're a clever/ lovely/enthusiastic/[insert the words they used here] person?

- What do you do that makes them think that? What do you say?

If you have words or phrases you frequently use in conversation, write them down. If you're really good at breaking the ice with a story or joke, write that down. If you can capture people's imaginations by painting vivid mental images, write that down.

You want to capture this verbal flavour in your written words. Then if someone goes to your website or gives you a call after reading your book, they will have a consistent experience of who you are.

Inviting your readers in

The language you use is a powerful tool – it can either make your knowledge accessible to others, or it can lock it away in a tomb guarded by indecipherable hieroglyphics. By writing in plain English you invite your readers into your world, gain their trust and give them the opportunity to benefit from your expertise. By falling back on jargon or academic writing, you push them away and make it less likely that they will contact you in future for other services.

Meanwhile, your personality is the element that sets you apart in your field. By giving yourself permission to be yourself, you'll also have a book that stands out from every other one in your industry.

The last step is to write it!

LANGUAGE WORKSHEET

1. To get an outsider's perspective on your unique personality traits, ask your clients, colleagues, friends and family the following questions:

   - How would they describe you to someone else?

   - What makes you different to everyone else they know?

   - Why do they like working with you?

2. Incorporate these qualities into your writing by asking your network:

   - Why do they think you're a clever/lovely/ enthusiastic/[insert the words they used here] person? What do you do that makes them think that? What do you say?

   - Write down the words and phrases you frequently use as well as the way you best engage others (such as sharing stories, jokes, or action hero references). Where could you incorporate these in your book?

3. When you start writing, remember to keep it simple with the following rules:

   - Omit needless words.

   - Never use a long word when a short one will do.

- Avoid the passive voice.
- Use contractions liberally.
- Write like you talk.
- Refer to yourself as 'I' and your reader as 'you'.
- Write so a twelve-year-old could understand.

Where to from here?

If you've made it to this chapter, you should now have a 3,000- to 5,000-word plan for your book.

Congratulations!

Most people don't get this far. They either don't plan at all, or they start planning and then get so excited about writing that they stop planning after just one or two chapters so they can dive into the writing process. Unfortunately, while they then have one or two great chapters, the rest have a weak structure and are light on content.

But not you – by pushing through where most would give up or get distracted, you now have:

- An idea you're passionate about, which you can write about knowledgeably, and which your target readers want to read about.

- A structure that answers your readers' top three questions: 'what', 'why' and 'how'. Not only will they quickly understand your content, but they will recognise why it's important and how they can implement your advice and get the results they want.

- Content that builds your credibility, proves your ideas, and persuades your reader.

- Language that sets your book apart from every other book in your field.

With this plan you won't be left sitting at your desk, watching a blinking cursor and waiting for inspiration to strike. You won't find yourself going off on tangents and writing filler content to boost your word count. And you won't have to go through round after round of editing, spending months on end and thousands more dollars than is necessary to get your book right.

Instead, you will be guided every step of the way. You have an outline of the content you need and how it should be organised. Inspiration, filler content and excessive editing won't be required.

All that's left is for you to write.

This is the next area where a lot of entrepreneurs trip themselves up.

Some think, 'I've already done so much work. There's not much left, so a break won't hurt.' They're wrong. A break *can* hurt. How many ideas have you had that you put aside so you could focus on 'more important things', only to forget them entirely or to never find the time to return to them?

The best time to write is *now*, while your motivation is high. If now isn't possible, then schedule a time that you will dedicate to writing. You might go to the country, lock yourself in a cabin and make it your full-time job for a couple of weeks. Or you might commit to writing an hour a day or a certain number of words a day for thirty days, either getting up early, staying up late, using your lunch break or using your commute.

Better yet, set a deadline. A great way to do this is to contact an editor or a self-publishing company to schedule your book for editing – that way you're not only accountable to yourself but you're accountable to them, too.[44]

Other entrepreneurs think, 'I'm just going to do a bit more research first.' There's a fine line between acquiring the knowledge required and procrastination. If this is how you feel after mapping out your book, then I'd guess it's the latter.

You've just finished reading a book about writing a book. You don't need to read another one – there's enough here to get you started. Likewise, you don't need to start researching self-publishing and everything that happens after you finish writing – wait until you have finished the first draft. When we get too far ahead of ourselves it's very easy to stop doing what needs to be done now. Instead, focus on your immediate task, and trust that all of that information and all of those experts will still be out there to answer your questions when you're ready to move ahead with the next stage.

---

44   Even better, pay a deposit. Things become much more motivating when money's on the line.

If you're worried about missing something, remember that this is just your first draft – you can always go back to Google on the second.

Then there are those entrepreneurs who think, 'Oh God – now I have this plan, it's real. I don't think I'm ready for this.' Honestly, you'll probably never be ready. But what sets great entrepreneurs apart from the rest is that they muster their courage, conquer their fears and make that all-important leap of faith.

You don't need to be ready to be an author or to commit yourself to writing a revolutionary book. All you need to do is commit to the first draft. Once you have the words on the page, you have something that you and your editor can work with. But *you're* responsible for getting those words on the page.

It doesn't need to take long. It doesn't need to cause a lot of stress. And you don't need to write a lot. But you *do* need to write.

So take this moment to commit – commit to writing an imperfect first draft. Commit to writing, even when you think you don't know enough. Commit to setting aside an hour a day for thirty days.

Commit to writing an awesome book.

Acknowledgements

To my parents, Louise and Bill, who encouraged me to read and write from a young age, despite concerns that I might grow up to become a starving artist – thank you for teaching me to dream big, and to believe that 'good enough' isn't good enough.

To Gavin Bunshaw, who spurred my leap into entrepreneurship. I'm not sure you'll ever realise how big an impact you've had on my journey – if it weren't for our thirty-minute chat about my future a few years ago, I have no idea where I'd be today.

To my original editor Carolyn Jackson – I know that editing the boss's book must have been an intimidating prospect, and I'm so grateful you were up to the challenge. Thank you for giving me the feedback I needed to write a much better book.

To my publishing team – Michael Hanrahan for catching all of the little errors I was too lazy to correct myself, Scarlett Rugers for the brilliant cover and internal layout and Nick and Vivienne Kane at Excite Print who turned the digital files into physical books – I wouldn't have a book without you, so a big thank you!

To Andrew Griffiths, Glen Carlson and the rest of the KPI program – thank you for giving so many entrepreneurs the framework to get published, and for helping me discover my internal 'chatter' around my publishing journey.

Finally, to my partner, Andrew Martin – I know how challenging it can be for someone with his feet on the ground to live with someone with her head in the clouds. Thank you for holding strong through my business journey so far, from the peaks of giddy excitement when I signed new clients and unearthed new ideas, to the crashes when I lost faith, money and sleep. I doubt I would have gotten this far without your support, so thank you. I love you.

About the author

Jacqui Pretty is the Founder and Head Editor of Grammar Factory, a writing, editing and coaching company that helps entrepreneurs write awesome books.

She has a Bachelor of Arts with a major in Professional Writing and Editing from Monash University and over eight years of professional writing and editing experience. Since the launch of Grammar Factory in 2013, she and her team have worked with over 100 authors across a range of industries – including business, finance, health and wellness, travel, marketing, property, hospitality, law, photography, personal development and more.

Although Jacqui's clients had a mountain of knowledge to share, she continued to encounter the same issues in the books she edited. Often their structures were convoluted, their content was repetitive and there were large gaps in the authors' arguments, leading her to make thousands of changes and cut thousands of words.

What frustrated Jacqui was that all of these issues could have been dealt with in the writing process, and this set her on a journey to create a system that any entrepreneur could use to write an awesome book, regardless of their writing experience. That system became the backbone of her *Book Blueprint* workshops and book, and is the same system she used to draft her book in just three days.

Jacqui has been invited to speak as a writing and publishing expert by The Entourage, Australia's largest educator and community of entrepreneurs, and the Key Person of Influence program, dubbed 'The world's leading personal brand accelerator' by *The Huffington Post*.

Many of her clients have become Amazon bestsellers, been featured on national television, landed paid speaking engagements and doubled their revenue. In short, she has witnessed first-hand the power of publishing to transform a business.